A
HISTORY
OF
CRICKET
IN
HAMPSHIRE

Norman Gannaway

HAMPSHIRE BOOKS

First published in 1990 by Hampshire Books

ISBN 1 871940-04-4

British Library Cataloguing-in-publication Data
Gannaway, Norman
A history of cricket in Hampshire.
1. Hampshire. Cricket history
I. Title
796.358094227

Printed and bound in Great Britain by BPCC Wheatons Ltd

HAMPSHIRE BOOKS
Official Publisher to Hampshire County Council

An imprint of Wheaton Publishers Ltd
A member of Maxwell Communication Corporation plc

Wheaton Publishers Ltd
Hennock Road, Marsh Barton, Exeter, Devon EX2 8RP
Tel: 0392 411131   Fax: 0392 425274

SALES
Direct sales to Hampshire Books at the address above

A Message from Mark Nicholas,
Captain of Hampshire County Cricket Club

IT IS WITH GREAT PLEASURE that I write a few words in *A History of Cricket in Hampshire*. Although cricket is played in every corner of Hampshire, it is the County team that sets the mood and standard for those at the grass roots to follow.

Hampshire, of course, has been a host to a wide variety of cricket, players and characters. They have entertained and infuriated the County's faithful with miracles and mediocrity, poetry and pathos. No county can have so inconsistently balanced the ingredients of success and failure, magic and motivation that were first cultured by Lord Tennyson, unparalleled by Colin Ingleby-Mackenzie and revisited by a team that boasts the flair and genius of Marshall, Gower and Robin Smith.

Interestingly, the rich tradition spread from the playing fields to the corridors of administration. Hampshire's contribution to cricket's nerve centre, the M.C.C., is second to none.

Sir Francis Lacey (cricket's first knight) started the trend as secretary of the M.C.C. in 1898. Since then Harry Altham, Ronnie Aird and Cecil Paris have been treasurers, secretaries and presidents between them, Cecil Paris succeeding Prince Philip in 1975.

When one considers that Captain T.O. Jameson, Major E.G. Wynyard and former County captains Ingleby-Mackenzie, Richard Gilliat and Nick Pocock have all served the M.C.C. at committee or administrative levels, one begins to get a clearer idea of the extent of Hampshire's link with the great club.

Talking of links, I doubt there is a county which boasts a finer array of cricketers from overseas. In modern times four outstanding West Indians, Greenidge, Roy Marshall, Roberts and Malcolm Marshall, have given Hampshire cricket a power and belief born of Caribbean instinct and enthusiasm.

My personal favourite from abroad, the South African Barry Richards, had such elegance, such sophistication, that it is hard to think of a sportsman who brought more artistry to his arena. Lucky Hampshire!

I can hardly think of an era in the County's history that has not produced some precious jewels. Maybe that is why people feel so nostalgic about Hampshire's cricket; it somehow embodies so much of the charm of the summer game. This book is about Hampshire cricket's history; I hope I can play a part in ensuring the future.

Acknowledgements

Photographs are reproduced by kind permission of the following:

B. Bird: plate xii

E.P. Eagar: plate ix (lower)

David Frith and Lutterworth Press: plate v (lower), from *The Golden Age of Cricket, 1890-1914*, by David Frith

Isle of Wight County Press: plate xxiii (lower)

Roy Jackman: plate xix (lower)

Marylebone Cricket Club: plates ii (lower) and iv (lower)

Adrian Murrell: cover photograph of Robin Smith

Portsmouth and Sunderland Newspapers Ltd: plate xviii (lower)

Simon Rowley (of Burley): plate xvii (lower)

Southern Evening Echo: plates i (lower, photograph by Tony Mardell), xxi, xxii (upper) and xxiv (both photographs)

Foreword

MY FIRST CONTACT WITH Hampshire cricket was forty years ago, through my father-in-law, who lived in Boldre, near Lymington.

He much preferred fishing and regarded my liking for cricket with an astonished tolerance which did him credit. However, he decided that I ought to do something during August which would keep me happy even if he did not understand why.

He therefore arranged for me to meet John Reddy, who was then the Lymington captain. I had, of course, taken the precaution of bribing the secretary of the club for which I usually played to say what a splendid all-rounder I was. Even though this cost me more than I could afford, it usually ensured me one game, though seldom a second.

John asked me if I had a car. When I told him, truthfully, that I was saving up for one (as indeed I was still doing some years later) he shook his head and replied that in that case he could only manage to fit me in for home matches, if someone was injured. Fortunately for me, two Lymington players sustained unpleasant injuries from cider and I was asked to make up the numbers at the last minute.

Only w hen I reached the ground did I discover that I was to play in a charity match, against a side which contained many of the current Hampshire team.

After the visitors had scored about 300, John Reddy, who was a realist, insisted that the first seven of our batsmen should wear their pads. When the first wicket fell, he asked me if I would like to bat next. I declined. 'Good', he answered, 'off you go then.'

I believe that Shackleton was bowling at one end and Cannings at the other. Not that it mattered much as I failed to score from either during an innings which lasted twenty minutes, although each of them, as this was a charity game, bowled a series of dreadful balls in a vain effort to persuade me to score.

Finally, David Shackleton made the mistake of bowling a straight ball, which removed all the stumps and the wicketkeeper's smile when the ball hit him. As I walked away from the field hoping that nobody would know who I was, some idiot, over the tannoy system, which had previously been indistinct and was temporarily perfect, commented: 'Thank you, Denys Roberts, for an entertaining innings.'

A few years later, I bought a house in Wimborne. Almost every summer for the next twenty-five years I spend a couple of weeks there on holiday, arranging matters so that I was able to watch one or two of the matches which were played by the County at Bournemouth.

My memory of what I saw may well be inaccurate, but I recall the warm summer days, the sounds of subdued applause and the friendliness which seemed to infect the players as much as the spectators. I do not suppose that the crowds ever exceeded 3000 or so and somehow the County managed to retain the cheerful warmth of a club fixture in all the first class matches which I saw there.

For these memories, I shall always be in the debt of Hampshire, as indeed the reader will be to Norman Gannaway, who has compiled such an excellent history of cricket in the County.

I was reminded of many pleasant days in Hampshire by Patrick Eagar, the son of Desmond, captain and secretary of Hampshire C.C.C. for many years. Patrick was supposed to take a photograph of me for the Benson and Hedges Final brochure. He failed, after two reels, to take anything sufficiently flattering but looked very much like his father, whenever he laughed.

Denys Roberts
President, M.C.C. (1990)

Contents

Introduction

A HISTORY OF CRICKET IN HAMPSHIRE sets out to convey something of the game at all levels within the county over a period of more than 300 years. The aim has been to cover the ground in as representative a way as possible, depending to a large extent on the availability of sources of information. There will be omissions, difficult to avoid in a work of limited length. While every care has been taken to ensure accuracy, it is accepted that few areas of information are infallible, and versions of the same event do vary from time to time. While facts and figures are very much part of cricket, this book has sought also to express something about the character and development of the game in Hampshire.

With regard to county boundaries, local government reorganization in 1974 'transferred' the areas of Bournemouth and Christchurch from Hampshire into Dorset. For the purposes of this history, those places are regarded as very much part of Hampshire.

Thanks are due to a number of people who have contributed to the research and writing of this book in a variety of ways. Hampshire County Librarian, John Beard, has from the outset shown valued interest and encouragement. Others within the County Library who have given much appreciated help include Frances Bassett, Michael Beesley, Carol Crossland, Derek Dine, Pam Dunn, Greta Forrest, Keith Hayward, Barrie Kempthorne, Alan King, John Reynolds, Jackie Ryder, Philippa Stevens and John Thorn. Among others who have been most helpful in the making available of key material have been Peter Ashton, Arthur Holt, James Ellis, Jimmy James and Sarah Penny. Personal thanks are due to the author's wife, Evelyn Gannaway, for her constant encouragement of all that he has attempted in the field of sport, research and writing. Cricket conversation is an often unique source of knowledge, and much has been gained over the years through listening to cricketers such as Jack Barrett, Lew Gregory, Arthur Holt, John Stanley and Jack White.

The author is most appreciative of the Foreword so kindly written by Sir Denys Roberts, President of the M.C.C., and of the message contributed by Hampshire County Cricket Captain, Mark Nicholas, whose own qualities have been required to the full during successive last-ball wins, over Leicestershire and then Essex, in this season's Nat. West Trophy one-day matches.

This history is dedicated to those who have throughout the centuries put into Hampshire cricket very much more than they have ever taken out.

Norman Gannaway
Lymington, Hants.
1990

8

1

Beginnings

CRICKET HAD ITS BEGINNINGS in a hundred different places, in Kent, Surrey, Hampshire, Sussex, in London, on country village greens. You cannot trace the history of the game as emanating from a common origin. The nearest you can get is to follow its story in existing local records, county by county.

Hampshire cricket is fortunate as there is a wealth of the kind of local material to which Eric Parker refers above.

The origins of cricket have long been a subject of conjecture; some claim it goes back beyond the earliest written records. Some suggest the game had its roots in mankind's basic need to eat in order to survive. Skills necessary in the hunt were developed until they became an end in themselves. Competitions were the next stage. The impulse to throw and to catch, added to the striking with a stick at a still moving object such as a stone or ball, is the basis of many sports.

The earliest known reference to cricket is thought by many to date from the year 1300, derived from the Wardrobe Accounts of King Edward the First, as revealed in 1787 by the London Society of Antiquaries. There is mention in the 'Accounts' of playing 'creag', believed to relate to a form of cricket, played at Newenden in Kent. In time the game spread, initially throughout south-eastern England, then across into Hampshire.

The first generally accepted reference to cricket in Hampshire is contained in a descriptive Latin poem 'De Collegio', written in 1647 by Robert Mathew during what are believed to have been his last months as a student at Winchester College. At a time when college conditions have been described as 'severe', recreation was taken at the top of 'Hills', St Catherine's Hill outside Winchester. Winchester scholars went in fine weather twice daily, before breakfast and after dinner, to 'Hills' for the playing of games. Here, Robert Mathew's poem tells us, a form of football and cricket or baseball were played. Football of a kind is said to have been played at Winchester College as early as 1550, and in Robert Mathew's lines we have what is recognized as a positive reference to that sport.

Also of Winchester interest, Thomas Ken (later Bishop Ken) is said to have wielded a 'cricket batte' during his college days. Elected as a scholar at Winchester during September 1651, and admitted the following January, Thomas

Ken left a legacy at the college in the form of his name cut in a cloister, with the date, 1656. Apart from these facts connected with Winchester College very little is known about seventeenth-century cricket in Hampshire. However, the game would surely have been played in town and village, as it was in Kent, Sussex and Surrey. Incidents from those counties have attracted public mention but Hampshire seems less well served.

While positive cricket references are comparatively few during the 1600s, John Ford in *Cricket: A Social History 1700-1835* contends that from scattered evidence it is clear that cricket was fairly widely played for more that a century before 1700. Cricket was then a game for the young and poor rather than for those of wealth and rank as it would become during the eighteenth century, a period in which matches would attract growing attention.

Cricket, as an organized game, can be traced from around 1700. References to the sport begin to increase, with a full description of a cricket match appearing during 1706 in a Latin poem by William Goldwin. In the early eighteenth century newspapers were scarce, and much cricket would have been played without making press mention. During this time of limited recognition, cricket was itself changing. We have evidence relating to the game's pitches and implements, enough to show a time of adaption to altering needs.

Reference is made to the cricket ball by Edward Phillips (a nephew of John Milton) in his poem of 1658 *The Mysteries of Love*. It would be almost a further hundred years before mention is made of the ball's 'crimson' colour, again in a poem. In 1744 the ball's weight was specified as being between 5 and 6 oz.

The earliest known cricket bat dates from 1729. It weighed 2lb. 4oz., was shaped like a hockey stick except with a broader blade, and belonged to Mr John Chitty. This historic bat is inscribed 'J.C. 1729'. Leg guards were introduced around 1800, with other protective equipment at a later date still.

Of the wicket G.D. Martineau in *Bat, Ball, Wicket and All* states that its evolution can be traced back for some 250 years with the aid of recorded history. Beyond that it becomes a matter of deduction. The wicket in 1702 was believed to have measured 22 in. high and 6 in. wide, having two stumps and one bail. Around 1775-6 a third stump was added, although not universally adopted for a few years.

From the 1727 Articles of Agreement governing matches between teams of the Second Duke of Richmond and Mr Brodrick of Peper Harow, it can be seen that the pitch length, wicket to wicket, was 23 yd. In the 1744 Laws of Cricket reference is made to 22 yd. Playing surfaces were certainly not of the standard that later generations would expect!

Against this background of change, cricket developed in Hampshire. In late season 1729, at Penshurst Park, Kent, seat of the Earl of Leicester, the combined strength of Hampshire, Surrey and Sussex, headed by Sir William Gage, met Kent, led by Mr Edwin Stead, for 100 guineas a side. Kent were defeated before a crowd of some thousands, with a groom of the Duke of Richmond highly praised for his part in the win. The groom 'signalised himself by such extraordinary agility and dexterity' that "tis reckoned he turned the scale of victory which for some years has been generally on the Kentish side.' A return match was played at Lewes, scene, in 1694, of a 2s. 6d. wager on a game of cricket. Betting would become very much a feature of cricket's growth years.

John Ford considers that 'the period 1720-1835 coincided with the high point of gambling in this country.' Mr Ford believes that the development of cricket can only be clearly understood if the evidence of gambling throughout society is understood. Hampshire's cricket history provides instances of the part that betting played. In the 1740s, Slindon, main centre of Sussex cricket during the mid-eighteenth century, provided 1741 opposition for Portsmouth. In 1749 Portsmouth Common was the setting for a match at Mill Dam between those living on the Common against a side from Fareham and Titchfield. Also during 1749, at the Artillery Ground of Finsbury, where admission charges were made from 1744 and possibly earlier, 'Long Robin' with a gentleman from Havant was matched against two gentlemen of near Winchester for the sum of 40 guineas.

Dating also, it is thought, from 1749 is a painting 'Gentlemen v. Players at Brading, Isle of Wight', attributed to Francis Hayman. Once in the collection of Sir Jeremiah Colman, the painting, size 47 1/2 in. by 25 3/4 in., is rich in detail. 'In the far distance,' Eric Parker describes, 'is Spithead with a battle-ship, in the middle distance Brading with its churches, on the left a country inn, and on one of the far sides of the ground tents with the Union Jack and White Ensign.'

David Jarrett in *England in the Age of Hogarth* regards cricket as a sport 'that traditionally brought together the highest and the lowest in the land.' There is evidence that this was so in Hampshire. From this union, apart from their value in recording progress of the sport, writings from the later eighteenth century tell us much about those who took part in, watched and influenced Hampshire cricket. The Hambledon years, from the 1750s until the century's end, are of increasing interest in Hampshire and beyond, and give us considerable information about cricket and the county at large.

2

The Hambledon Years

HAMBLEDON CRICKET CLUB AND the part it played not only in Hampshire but throughout the game as a whole has provided material for countless books, articles and debates. For a summary of the role that Hambledon assumed we might turn to the opening paragraph of *The Hambledon Cricket Chronicle, 1772-1796*, by F.S. Ashley-Cooper, with an introduction by E.V. Lucas, published in 1924. Mr F.S. Ashley-Cooper writes:

> The story of the Hambledon Club is one of the most remarkable in the whole history of cricket. How a village organisation should have developed into such prominence, unchallenged and unchallengeable, and have been supported in its almost inaccessible quarters at Broad-halfpenny by most of the chief contemporary patrons, will always remain a mystery. If Hambledon cannot strictly be regarded as 'The Cradle of Cricket', it can at least claim to have been the centre in which the game was first brought to a certain degree of perfection and was developed in several respects to its lasting advantage.

The *Chronicle* not only gives us valuable contemporary background from newspaper reports and other sources, but information regarding 'The Match List 1772-1796', club accounts, membership, players, officers, supporters and patrons. The names have become legendary: the Revd Charles Powlett; Richard Nyren; William Beldham; the Revd Cotton; the treasurer, John Richards; the steward, Philip Husted, John Nyren; and the intriguing 'Madge', to whose 'immortal memory' toasts were drunk.

The grounds, Broad-halfpenny Down and then Windmill Down, 'on the hill and within about half a mile of the village', have become enshrined in the Hambledon legend. F.S. Ashley-Cooper sets the scene of the well-attended matches:

> It is pleasant to picture the thousands thronging the hill to the ground, the Duke of Dorset, Earls Tankerville and Winchilsea and others each with his coach and four, the players, farmers, etc., on horseback, and the great majority in vehicles of various kinds - a living stream of cricket enthusiasm. On Broad-

halfpenny itself would be refreshment booths, a special tent for 'the quality', and others for the players and the ladies.

Of cricket costume, we have quotes from the *Hampshire Chronicle* of July 1791, recording that 'The gentlemen of the Hambledon Club were uniformly dressed in sky-blue coats with black velvet collars, and the letters C.C. (Cricketing Club) engraved on their buttons.' Of betting, a major feature at the time, John Nyren was later to state that bets 'were always made for £500 aside'. The surviving Hambledon minute books have a fascination of their own. There is mention of cricket, wine, ballots for membership, club orders, the weather, settling of disputes. On 10 May 1774 it was:

Ordered: That if any dispute shall arise amongst the Members should they not be silent after being desired to waive the subject of conversation by the President or in his absence by the Stewards the gentleman so disputing shall forfeit one Doz: of Claret to the Club.

The Hambledon Minutes are often concerned with matters that would occupy village and town clubs some two hundred years later. In late September 1787 it was 'Ordered that grass seeds be sown on the Cricket ground this Autumn and that the Ground be rolled and beaten all the Winter.' As is to be expected there is debate over decision-making. In 1791 'The Umpire said; I really think the ball hit the Ground but I cannot be positive ...' Latter-day clubs often have men and women of note among their ranks. Hambledon on the 29 August 1796 recorded 'Mr Thos Pain, Authour of the rights of Man' as present with three members and twelve non-subscribers.

Hambledon's accounts include lists of gentlemen subscribers, details of the considerable numbers of wines and other drinks that were part of the scene and, in August 1796, 'Garrett for the rent of The Down - 10 10 0'. The match list 1772-96 tells the strength of opposition: England, Surrey, Kent, 22 of Liphook* and District, Farnham.

Of Hambledon's 1 wicket defeat in 1773 at the Artillery Ground, the *Reading Mercury* is quoted to the effect that 'There were about 20,000 spectators ... the last two for England went in for 19 notches, 8 of which they got by Lumpy, and the remainder by Miller.'

The Hambledon membership roll has many well-known names. From the barest details: 'Aberdeen. —; e 1776'; to the fuller: the 8th Earl of Winchilsea, 'the chief founder of the M.C.C. in 1787'; there are many paths that invite exploration. There is often colourful information about 'the players': William Barber, William Fennex, Andrew Freemantle, the Nyrens, Richard Veck, and the Smalls. The

---

*When the strongest clubs met those of lesser strength, the weaker opposition was often allowed to play more than eleven men, the numbers varying from fifteen to eighteen to twenty-two on occasions.

Chronicle sets out the Revd Reynell Cotton's 'Cricket Song for the Hambledon Club, Hants, 1767', with lines ranging from excitement, 'Ne'er a contest was seen with such fear and such joy', to the plainly sad 'For the Heroes of Cricket, like others, must die.' Desmond Eagar, a Hampshire captain who relished thought of the Hambledon days, writes of them:

> These were the men who brought immortal fame to the Hampshire village, who could hold their own with any team in England, and whose captain could proudly proclaim that it was never safe to 'bet your money against such men as we are'.

Hampshire cricket is much indebted for all that F.S. Ashley-Cooper's *The Hambledon Cricket Chronicle* provides. E.V. Lucas in *The Hambledon Men*, first published 1907, reprinted during 1954, brings us the writings of John Nyren, the Revd John Mitford, The Revd James Pycroft and others. *From Hambledon to Lords's: The Classics of Cricket*, edited by John Arlott, is also rich in the works of such writers. One notable example is Hambledon's victory in June 1777 over All England, with 167 runs from James Aylward, according to Arthur Haygarth 'one of the few cricketers there are who from first to last continued the game for 30 seasons.'

Hambledon's fame was very much an encouragement to cricketers in other parts of the county. Over towards the Dorset border, Bisterne, whose William Mills was elected to Hambledon membership in 1787, made an announcement in 1781:

> Tis to be hoped this noble game by the generous patronage of the sire, together with the knowledge and good example of the 2 young men in this exercise, will tho' but very lately in those parts, enable their countrymen to rival the boasted champions of Broad Halfpenny.

Through John Goulstone's *Early Club and Village Cricket*, we have a valuable informative checklist of first known dates (from the eighteenth century, with many falling within the Hambledon years) for venues and clubs throughout Hampshire. John Goulstone has researched sources such as F.S. Ashley-Cooper, Arthur Haygarth, H.T. Waghorn, G.B. Buckley, H.F. and H.P. Squire, as well as a wide range of books, periodicals and newspapers. In addition to the bare facts, John Goulstone has a number of brief illuminating comments. At Newport, Isle of Wight, in 1788, 'A weekly cricket match is established between the gentlemen of the Island. On the day of playing they dine together in the greatest harmony.' When Hambledon visited Itchen Stoke Downs in 1788, Richard Nyren of The George, Hambledon, provided the refreshments and also advertised that he had:

... a stock of excellent wines and cold provisions, and hopes the air of Stoke Down will, with the ladies at least, stand in the place of marbres, aspiques, blancmanges, &c. For good appetite there will be a sufficient quantity of beef, ham, chicken and tarts.

John Goulstone has found early mention of places as wide apart as Barton Down, Cosham, Odiham, Netley Marsh, Hursley, Totton, Gosport, Compton, Alresford, Bishop's Waltham, Wherwell, Alton, Southampton, Andover and Portsmouth.

There has been prolonged debate concerning the date of Hambledon's rise to prominence. Much attention has been paid to James Pycroft's quote of William Beldham's comment:

If you want to know, sir, the time the Hambledon Club was formed, I can tell by this - when we beat them in 1780, I heard Mr Paulett say, 'Here have I been thirty years raising our Club, and we to be beaten by a mere parish?'

A number of authorities have settled on 1756 as an agreed date for Hambledon's start, a year in which the club met Dartford.

There is less doubt regarding Hambledon's decline. Harry Altham comments:

The founding of the M.C.C. in 1787 was really the death-knell of the Hambledon Club: more and more did London become the centre of great cricket, and steadily the membership declined, and the players were lured away by the golden magnet.

The final entry in the Hambledon Club Minutes, the year 1796, reads: 'Sepr 21st - No Gentlemen.'

3

Seasons of Change

THE YEARS FROM 1800 saw considerable changes in the pattern of Hampshire cricket. There were periods when the game clearly flourished. Against this were times when sport struggled for survival. There were wars abroad and troubles at home. Hampshire entered the 1800s with a population of some 200 000, with communities in many parts of the county in relative isolation from others. Cricket was in some ways a unifying force, despite the spirit in which matches were often played. Cricket in 1800 had to compete for newspaper space with accounts of war on the Continent and unrest in Britain. Food riots during 1800 were experienced in Portsmouth over 'excessively high price of provisions' and at Fareham and Romsey, while at Southampton a mob assembled to seize butter and potatoes. A summer in which 'such a long interval of dry and intensely hot weather is not remembered' would not have helped.

Troop movements and related rumours were much in the news. April 1800 had Southampton, with a population of around 8000, hearing that a camp for 30 000 men was to be formed in the vicinity. The Prince of Orange's troops of 5000 were in the Isle of Wight,where the Northwood Parish Register for 1801-1802 showed records of many foreign troops who had died there, often as a result of wounds suffered in the French Revolutionary wars. Porchester Castle in 1800 held upward of 5000 prisoners of war. The *Hampshire Chronicle* on 14 September 1801 stated that 'according to report, all persons capable of service, from the age of sixteen to sixty, are to be armed with pikes in the districts along the coast most liable to any sudden descent of the enemy.'

Against this background, Hampshire cricket during 1801 made a limited impact. Places to stage matches, with betting a popular feature, including Micheldever, Alresford, Romsey, Hursley, Bishopstoke, Redbridge and Portsmouth. The setting of an August sun saw play between East Meon and Stoke against Hambledon 'postponed *sine die*', which on occasions meant the following season.

In the early 1800s, Robert 'Long Bob' Robinson, a Hampshire player from 1792 to 1816, experimented with a leg-guard of thin angled, protective board. In the face of laughter from others, Robinson apparently 'gave up his armour' and it was several decades before pads came into general use.

In an 1802 season of May frosts and mixed weather into the summer, Winchester's match with Hampshire at Twyford Down in mid-September was scheduled to begin at 9 o'clock. The 'County' made 27 and 49, victors Winchester 68 and 9 for 1 wicket. At Peartree Green, Itchin (*sic*) Ferry XI defeated Southampton by an innings.

Hampshire during 1803 visited Lord's to meet the combined strength of Nottinghamshire and Leicestershire. At Peartree Green, 'a vast concourse attended, and booths were stationed with cold collations and every sort of liquor for the entertainment of the parties and their friends' to watch Itchen Ferry successful once more against Southampton.

In April 1803 a letter from Havre to a gentlemen of Southampton expressed concern at hearing:

... of the preparations that are going forward on your side of the water. We wait with anxious expectation to know the event. There is nothing preparatory to war going on here, and I will undertake to say that the whole of the French at this time are quite averse to going to war with England.

May 1803 saw renewal of England's war with France.

In a cricket match running over from 1803 into 1804, Winchester defeated Heckford on Twyford Down to complete a task begun the previous year. Also victorious in 1804 were Hampshire, at Lord's against the Marylebone and Homerton club.

The Revd Lord Frederick Beauclerk, a colourful character in cricket history, featured prominently in Hampshire's fixtures during 1805 with All England. Said to have made 600 guineas a year from betting at cricket, Lord Beauclerk is reputed to have placed a gold watch on his wicket when at practice, as inducement to the bowlers. An early reference to wide bowling comes from an account of a notable single-wicket contest of 1810 involving Lord Beauclerk and T.C. Howard of Hartley Wintney against 'Squire' Osbaldeston and William Lambert.

The appearance of Josia Jackson, recently returned from the West Indies and due to contest Southampton's next town election, in a field near Southampton's Polygon was greeted with 'huzzas'. Also near the Polygon, in Mr Antram's field, cricket was followed by festive sports and 'pugilism in the Mendoza style with stuffed gloves'.

Hampshire's score against All England in August 1806 was reported as 150 'notches'. The term 'run' had come into being at the beginning of the 1800s, but the use of 'notches' (derived from the keeping of scores by cutting notches on a stick) continued for some while. Hambledon in their summer of 1806 innings against Winchester were on record as having 'fetched' 144 runs.

Sawdust achieved recognition at Lord's on 27 June 1806 when in a successful attempt to take Lord Frederick Beauclerk's wicket in a single-wicket contest, Beldham took up a lump of wet earth and sawdust, stuck it to the ball, and then 'pitched favourably, made extraordinary twist and took the wicket'. A late September 1806 'famous cricket match' for 50 guineas saw Southampton's 37 and 83 too many for the 24 and 74 from Titchfield.

Cricket in 1807 saw first mention of the revival of straight-armed bowling, by John Willes of Kent. Also reflecting change, the *Hampshire Telegraph* of 3 August 1807 was using the modern letter 's', as well at retaining the older 'f'-like character for 's' in some parts of the edition.

In contrast to games extending at times into a week, on a Thursday in August 1808 at Stoke's Bay, Gosport, the Gentlemen of Portsmouth and Southsea, having beaten Gosport by 50 notches, at once set about a return match in which they were again the winners. All within a day, with bets 'depending to a considerable amount'. Betting very much in fashion, an 'expert runner' in October 1808 undertook, for a wager, to run 17 miles along the Winchester road in two hours, a feat 'he effected with great ease', having five minutes to spare.

There was clearly an audience for sporting contests. 'Not less, it is supposed, than 10 000 persons' gathered in May 1809 for rural sports and pastimes on Southsea Common. 'A match at single stick', four from Hampshire against four from Wiltshire, in the autumn of 1809, attracted a 'very numerous company'. Also drawing crowds later in 1809, were celebrations marking the fiftieth year of the reign of King George III. Reminding us of military presence in Hampshire at that date, Portsmouth Militia met during 1810 and defeated their Sussex counterparts at cricket by an innings and 8 runs.

At a time when concern was being expressed at the enclosure of wastelands, 'the more corn we grow, the less we shall need import' the advocates argued. Southsea Common was not only the scene of cricket involving Portsmouth, Horndean, Rowlands Castle, Compton and Clanfield, with much attendant betting, but also the venue for a duel that concluded happily without damage and with satisfaction that 'honor had not been tarnished'.

Hampshire women made their mark on cricket during 1811, defeating Surrey women at Newington. The *Hampshire Chronicle* of 7 October 1811 fielded a mid-match report:

The match was made between two amateur Noblemen of the respective counties, for five hundred guineas a side. The performers in this singular contest were of all ages and sizes, from 14 years old to upwards of 40; and the different parties were distinguished by coloured ribbons: royal purple for the Hampshire; orange and blue, Surrey. The weather being favourable on Wednesday, some very excellent play, and much skill were displayed; but the palm of this day was borne off by a Hampshire lass, who made 41 runs before she was thrown out. At the conclusion of the day, the first innings for

18

Hampshire were 81, while those of Surrey were only seven. Five to one on the Hampshire lasses; any odds offered, but no takers. Thursday the Surrey damsels kept the field with their second innings almost the whole of the day; but it rained so incessantly that there was very little play. The game, it is expected, will not be concluded until Monday next; but the general opinion is, that Hampshire will gain the victory. Notwithstanding the unfavourable state of the weather, a great concourse of people attended to witness this singular contention;...

For a late season 'Grand Final Cricket Match' at Clapham, admission 1s., Sarah Luff was billed to lead the Hampshire Ladies XI playing in 'True Blue', against the orange and blue of Surrey. At the end of November 1811 Portsmouth experienced an earthquake shock, similar in extent to the last shock during 1734. The *Hampshire Telegraph* of December 1811 reported: 'We deprecate these terrifying visits of nature, or of nature's God.'

Following an early season 1812 performance of Winchester Inhabitants against the Loyal Winchester Volunteers, it was hoped that the spirit present in the city would be 'productive of many matches'. Among clubs to take to the Hampshire field were The Bourne, Preston Candover, Winchester, Portsmouth, Newton Vallance and Hambledon. In August 1812, Winchester greeted accounts of Lord Wellington's 'glorious victory' with 'every mark of joy and satisfaction'.

Generally favourable weather during the summer of 1813 encouraged cricket in central and northern Hampshire, with four-a-side matches involving the Wells and Holloway families attracting particular attention.

Midsummer 1814 was met with celebrations at Reading of the Proclamation of Peace. Repercussions from the Napoleonic Wars, however, saw distress and lawlessness throughout the land. Nightly robberies became so frequent in parts of Hampshire 'that a universal consternation seems to prevail and no man retires to rest without pistols or some kind of arms by his bedside.' Cricket reports were relatively few, although Single Stick at Fareham attracted players from Hampshire, Wiltshire and Somerset.

The autumn of 1815 drew heat enough to burst a thermometer in the garden of Thomas Sharp at Romsey. Much Hampshire press comment was concerned with events in France, although cricket from places such as Holybourne, Alresford, Portsmouth, Apple Down, Andover, Wherwell, Longparish, Weyhill, Bighton, Sutton, Medstead and Preston Candover gained mention.

Cowes received Southampton at Mr Ward's ground during October 1816, and a week later staged a single-wicket contest in a field near the Horseshoe public house. William Ward, for some years a Member of Parliament for the City of London was a leading batsman of his time. Hampshire-qualified it is thought through owning property in the Isle of Wight, he was a major influence in the game playing a major part in saving Lord's for English cricket. A strong man who used a 4lb. bat William Ward made 278 for M.C.C. against Norfolk at Lord's in 1820 achieving the first double century and the highest innings on record at that time. The 1816 season saw Hampshire in opposition to the M.C.C., and Epsom, whose own cricket dated back to a 1730 match against Sunbury on Epsom Downs.

Drought in the early summer of 1817 ended with June rains 'so opportunely fallen' and one of the finest harvests within memory. Hampshire club cricket showed signs of steps forward. An Isle of Wight 'so full of company' staged frequent Gentlemen v. Players fixtures. A number of series (such as Havant against Emsworth and Southampton v. Lyndhurst) attracted betting interest in other parts of the county. Commitment would have seemed to the fore when Southampton Cabinet Makers (55 and 45) narrowly defeated Southampton Carpenters in a 'severe contest' with a 'great exertions on both sides'.

Hampshire's summer of 1818 brought a report that 'so intense heat of the weather has not been known these thirty years'. Goodwood Park provided worthy 1818 opposition and opportunity for heavy betting in meetings with clubs from the Portsmouth area. The Hampshire v. Sussex pigeon-shooting contest attracted a betting public, as did such an event on the Isle of Wight, itself enjoying the finest crops for forty years.

Marchwood women drew thousands of spectators to their Married v. Single cricket during midsummer 1819, the gathering including 'some of the first respectability and fashion'. Less favourably inclined towards women's activities was the *Sporting Magazine* 1819. Commenting on the waltz, then popular in parts of England, a magazine contributor wrote that: 'English women cannot waltz without doing violence to some invaluable notions of delicacy and reserve with which they have been brought up.'

Music was in the 1819 air. Following Hampshire's three-day victory over Surrey at Epsom: 'After dinner, Mr Dignum, the singer delighted the company with some good old songs on the manly game of cricket and several other sweet melodies.' The social side of cricket would develop considerably over the years, with food, drink and music very much part of the occasion. Apart from his innings of 278 for the M.C.C. against Norfolk at Lord's in 1820, William Ward is much reported during a career rich with interest. In 1825 Ward bought the remaining sixty-eight-year lease of Lord's Ground from Thomas Lord for £5000. On an occasion when batting at Lord's, William Ward played a ball into 'the inclosure of his pantaloons', posing a problem for the fielding side. In the field, on another day, he was himself party to an intriguing situation. During one of the experimental matches of 1827 to try out 'round arm' bowling, of which James Broadbridge of Sussex was a pioneer, Ward caught Broadbridge after that player had literally thrown his bat at the widest of deliveries. James Broadbridge, able to bat left or right handed and ready to walk 25 miles for a game of cricket, was not at all pleased with his dismissal.

Although the county side played only one match during 1821, there were reports of clubs at places such as Pennington, Cowes, Hilsea, Ryde, Hambledon, Portsdown, Stockbridge and Newport. The season was less than welcoming, with a cold June featuring 'severe hailstones', then August wind and rain strong enough to damage crops. The 'young club' at Southampton was, the *Hampshire Telegraph* of May 1821 claimed, in 'such a state of improvement, that they are supposed to be nearly equal to any juvenile club in England.'

At Sarisbury Green on Whit Tuesday 1821, the Singles in opposition to the Married of Titchfield had the incentive of playing for two and twenty sovereigns, plus a fat sheep, this to encouragement from an 'immense concourse' of spectators. The cook of the Marquis of Buckingham's yacht superintended roasting of the sheep, 'which was as fine a one as Dorsetshire could produce, and done as well as any single joint before a kitchen range.' The season was also memorable for Thomas Beagley, born at Farringdon near Alton, noted batsman and splendid longstop, his unbeaten 113 at Lord's being the first century achieved in a Gentlemen v. Players match. Having dismissed the Gentlemen for 60, the Players went on to 278 for 6 wickets, at which stage the Gentlemen 'gave up', according to Sir Pelham Warner 'a not uncommon practice in those days'. Of betting at that time, Sir Pelham supposed that bookmakers 'would not accept bets from players if they played for the side other than that which they had backed.' The 'selling' of matches was far from unknown.

Cricket had from 1822 the facility of match reporting in *Bell's Life* and *Annals of Sporting and Fancy Gazette*. Hampshire's own press comments were often intriguing. The *Southampton County Chronicle* in June 1822 reported a notice that on Whit Monday:

> The Amusement that was Calld Baddsley fair that was held at East End: will this year take place on Camiel Green Betwixt Norley Wood; and Bewley Railes, first That will be a Game of Cricketts and the next that will be half a dozen Girls to Run for Ribbons.

Ready to support local claims the same newspaper in May 1822 wrote: 'The umpires, Messrs Mitchel and Beagly, gave it as their decided opinion, that the Alresford eleven are competent to play any parish within 20 miles.'

Hampshire's summer of 1823 was unsettled enough to persuade the King to postpone his August visit to Cowes, but improved sufficiently by November for green peas to be growing in an Emsworth garden and an Odiham tree to bear a second crop of apples. Shortage of business at Hereford's August 1823 assizes encouraged Gentlemen of the Bar to obtain the use of a piece of land on which they played cricket. Improvising in a different manner, at races of the Yeomanry Corps, according to the *Hampshire Advertiser* of August 1823, one of the members rode a race smoking a cigar. He lost the race but kept the cigar alight.

Mary Russell Mitford, Alresford born in 1787, had her article 'The Cricket Match' published in the *Lady's Magazine* in 1823. Many a village in Hampshire might have endorsed Mary Russell Mitford's words from the lips of William Grey: 'We do not challenge any parish, but if we be challenged, we are ready.'

Mary Russell Mitford had, in her own life, known a wide variation of hardship and fortune. Parts of Hampshire during the mid-1820s knew deeply troubled times. Mr A. Temple Patterson's *A History of Southampton 1700-1914* reminds us of the lawlessness around 1824 and after. Of some solace, 'less injurious to others, but also condemned as irreligious or vicious, were the cricket-playing and gambling by boys and young men on the Marsh on Sunday mornings.'

Winchester College's first-ever match at Lord's, against Harrow on 27 and 28 July 1825, was widely reported for a disastrous fire that destroyed the pavilion during the second night. Not only were many unique records lost for ever, but the whole future of Lord's was in the balance. William Ward, an old Wykehamist cricketer, then stepped into the breach. Edmund H. Fellowes in *A History of Winchester Cricket* acknowledges that Thomas Lord's name is immortalized in the Ground, and reminds us that the name of William Ward should not be forgotten. Having won the first Harrow match by 139 runs, in the second Lord's meeting during 1826, Winchester were the winners by a margin of 384, thanks much to an undefeated 146 from William Meyrick. For the College's first encounter with Eton, at Lord's in 1826, Winchester players took the field wearing 'white duck trousers, a white jean jacket with pink, and a high hat'.

There is report of a decline in Hampshire cricket around 1825. True though this may be of some parts there was spirited play elsewhere. Of a meeting in 1825 between a Gentlemen of the New Forest XI against a Southampton XI, 'a more severe contest is not within the annals of cricket', this with a wager of 100 sovereigns at stake. Southampton made 46 and 57, the New Forest 56 and 48 for 7. The Royal Academy Observatory at Gosport recorded variable 1826 weather. Southampton racecourse endured a swarm of ladybirds. A storm at Lyndhurst was powerful enough to break 'nearly all the glass in the place'.

While play between Fareham and Bishop's Waltham at Waltham Chase in 1827 was described as 'very indifferent', the New Forest against Southampton match drew praise as 'the most interesting and well-played game in Hampshire for several years.'

Hampshire's County XI during 1828 played their last major match for fourteen years. Cricket elsewhere within the borders was in a relatively quiet phase, but despite this the *Hampshire Advertiser* carried an item headed 'Cricketing'. At Ringwood, although there were balls enough left by the disbanded cavalry, the club was in need of new bats. Of wider interest, an 1828 amendment of cricket's laws permitted a round-arm bowler now to raise his hand level with the elbow.

Despite May 1829 weather 'as cold as Christmas' in parts of Hampshire, and news of a smallpox outbreak, there was cricketing hope in the air. Several matches were spoken of at Southampton, 'and the noble game, which has so long been neglected, is to be revived with much spirit this season.' Cricket had to take second place to harvesting at Stockbridge for a while, as elsewhere. Hampshire's club reports from around 1829 began increasingly to include details of bowling and are much welcomed by later cricket researchers. The earliest generally accepted evidence of a full bowling analysis, including maiden overs, is attributed to an 1834 fixture between Yorkshire and Norfolk.

Transport was a key element in the growth of Hampshire cricket, not least with regard to the Isle of Wight. The increase in the availability of steam-packet passage opened up the exchange of fixtures between Island and mainland. Portsmouth Garrison were in August 1829 offered a friendly welcome by anxiously waiting hosts at Newport, then subjected to a heavy defeat (53 and 20, with no double-figure scores to the visitors; Newport 138) before a 'great concourse of spectators'.

The 'no ball', for long a bone of contention among cricketers and administrators, began to appear separately on score sheets from 1830. One of the most respected umpires of the 1830s was William Caldecourt from Hampshire, said to have officiated with his right arm tucked into his waistcoat. A ground boy at Lord's before becoming a practice bowler at the age of fifteen in 1818, in addition to being an umpire of high reputation, William Caldecourt had also been player, coach and groundsman. Patrick Morrah has written that 'no professional cricketer was more highly respected'.

'Nothing but enjoyment, and no mistake,' was written of Lyndhurst Amusements, revived in 1831. This might well have been true of Basingstoke's senior and junior musicians who not only met each other at cricket, but united to play their instruments 'through the principle streets' of the town that summer.

The Reform Act and various public festivals attracted Hampshire press interest during 1832. Also on a high note, the Winchester area wheat harvest: 'most abundant, was probably never got together in finer condition'. Compliments were in September 1832 at a Southsea cricket match extended to Mr Charles Swales, presented with a silver-mounted baton by members of the Portsmouth club, 'as a testimonial of esteem' for his 'valuable services during the season'. Some 150 years later 'Clubman of the Year' awards are fashionable, of which this was perhaps an early example.

Cricket literature was enriched in 1833 by the publication of John Nyren's *The Young Cricketer's Tutor* and *The Cricketers of My Time*, collected and edited by Charles Cowden Clarke. John Nyren, Hambledon born in 1764, son to Richard Nyren of Hambledon 'Bat and Ball Inn' and cricket fame, watched Hambledon cricket as a boy and with Charles Cowden Clarke brought to life men who were giants in that period of Hampshire cricket. In *The Cricketers of My Time* we read of wicketkeeper-batsman Tom Sueter, with 'an eye like an eagle, rapid and comprehensive', and about Thomas Brett, 'beyond all comparison, the fastest as well as the straightest bowler that was ever known'. Of Edward Aburrow, 'one of our best long fields' and 'beloved by all his acquaintances'. 'The Little Farmer' Lamborn perfected his art by bowling away for hours at a hurdle or two when tending his father's sheep. As well as cricket we are told of character. Men such as John Small, the elder, well versed in points of cricket law and talented enough on the violin to calm the anger of an enraged bull.

John Arlott writes of *The Cricketers of My Time* that it 'comes out of a deep enthusiasm which had become a faith, a nostalgia which was as searching as intense, and a certainty which comes of knowing a game as a craft and one's fellow-practitioners as human beings.'

Hampshire cricket reports of 1833 convey a strong sense of festival and community. The game was bringing something into the lives of those who took part and the many who watched. Among teams to share this phase in the county's play were Fair Oak, Ampfield, Andover, Overton, Boldre, Dummer, Newport, Brockenhurst and South Hants.

The season of 1834 met its share of difficulties. Late summer of 1834 brought reports of sudden deaths in Portsea and Landport, 'owing no doubt, to the extreme heat and the indulgence in fruit and cold liquids to an excess.' Some cricket clubs were ready to judge and advise their opponents. Having defeated Newport by 5 wickets in August 1834, Hambledon recommended that Newport practise a little more before giving thought to accepting another challenge. Brockenhurst for their part suggested that a beaten opposition 're-model the eleven' and 'practise well together'. Differences reached a high point during an 1834 fixture at Twyford Down. A Winchester batsman left the crease to assist an injured Alresford player, at which point another of the fielding side threw down the batsman's wicket and claimed a dismissal. The batsman chose to stay his ground, at which point the match ended in dispute, with some doubt cast as to the likelihood of its completion at a later date. Local pride was often strong, with very little given away.

England's troubles at home continued during 1835, with Hampshire experiencing the vagrancy (and the petty crime attributed to this) being met elsewhere. A summer of sometimes oppressive heat and severe drought did nothing to cool the public temper. At Alresford Autumn 1835 Petty Sessions, three men were convicted for an assault upon a Mr James Francis, returning from a cricket match between Basingstoke and Alresford at which an umpiring decision had led to crowd disturbance.

The umpire's lot through the years has rarely been a happy one. In 1835 they had to familiarize themselves with a revised Code of Laws. The bat's length was limited to 38 in., limitation of width dating from the early 1770s, while the follow-on was now compulsory after a deficit of 100 runs. During 1835 umpires became forbidden to bet on cricket matches.

Sussex County Cricket Club was formed during 1836, while in neighbouring

Hampshire, Southampton reported it 'gratifying to note that this truly English sport is so much patronised in this neighbourhood.' Reports came also of cricket involving Fawley, Eaglehurst, Stoney Cross, Mottisfont and Emsworth, while a Titchfield v. Fareham meeting of 'much friendliness' ended with 'the greatest hilarity' at the Bugle Inn.

Clubs were by now venturing further afield in search of fixtures, with Bedhampton meeting Chichester and Ringwood arranging a visit to Wimborne. 'Popping Crease' of the *Hampshire Advertiser* in September 1836 while writing of Fawley against Millbrook referred affectionately to 'our dear and gallant old England'. The *Advertiser* made a plea, echoed down the ages, for submission of match scores in good time for publication.

Following a mild winter, the cricket season of 1837 varied from snow and sleet in May to a settled August. Somerley C.C. was formed during 1837, playing in the grounds of Lord Normanton. Many village and estate teams were much indebted to landowners for the provision of pitches in this way.

The season of 1838 brought not only remarkable variations of weather, but also reports of intriguing events. A coppice near Cowes was showered with herring fry that covered trees and vegetation, the product of a water spout it was thought. Across the water, Christchurch's victory over Ringwood at Stanpit Marsh was celebrated with toasts, glees and singing. Some three thousand people gathered at Southampton's West End to watch women at cricket. On Southampton Common, reports of the Bugle's win over a French XI made mention of the scorers, Messrs Hayden and Walter. There was a press account of the laying of the first stone at Southampton Docks. Complaints about umpires were raised once more and the size of match balls was established at between 9 and 9 1/4 in. circumference.

During 1838 Hampshire County Cricket Club announced itself 'to appear again under the auspices of that excellent patron of the game Mr Chamberlayne'. On a visit to London, Hampshire with 90 and 99 defeated Marylebone's 100 and 42 by 47 runs. A County XI in 1838 also engaged to play Stonehenge. Other places to report cricket were Curdridge, Wellow, Ramsdean, Bramshaw, Steep and Basingstoke.

Mr Oakley opened a new cricket ground in Southampton during 1839, with every exertion made, it was claimed, to provide facilities able to rival those of Lord's. Practice nets were beginning to come into use at about that time. Of Hampshire's June 1839 win by 22 runs over Stonehenge at Cranbury Park, 'Aesop' quoted *Lillywhite's Book of Scores*: 'Though the winning side is called Hampshire, still it is presumed it can scarcely be the best eleven in the County. In fact, about this time there was no true Hampshire Eleven.' 'Aesop' contested this view: 'Hampshire had a very good Eleven, but they were not put together.'

Alan Edwards' *Milestones of Hampshire Cricket* is an invaluable source of Hampshire cricket dates from the earliest matches, and gives the first recorded mention of inter-Services cricket in the county to date from around 1840, when the Army played the Navy at Portsmouth. The Services have made a major contribution to Hampshire sport over the years. With regard to cricket, much will have stemmed from the Army Commander in Chief's Order, during 1841, that cricket grounds should be provided for each barracks station. This provision made available, in time, not only quality venues, but also a widening range of worthy opponents.

Another impact on cricket during the early 1840s, was the spread of the railway network throughout England. J.H. Bettey's *Wessex from AD 1000*, published in 1986, tells of a railway from London reaching Southampton in 1840, a branch of the London and Southampton Railway to Gosport during 1842, with Portsmouth and Salisbury having railways by 1847, the year in which the Southampton to Dorchester line ('Castleman's Corkscrew') took in Ringwood, Wimborne and Poole. Improved transport allowed cricket clubs to extend their range of fixtures, as well as enabling spectators to follow the teams. Portsmouth Cricket Club were glad in 1840 of attending support at their match with Porchester. Finding themselves below strength, Portsmouth recruited from among their followers, albeit that this 'did unfortunately take in some parties who knew nothing of the game.'

Hampshire cricket was much involved with the Antelope Ground at Southampton during the 1840s, made famous by the noted player: Daniel Day. Robert West has delved deeply into the background of Day's and other grounds. Robert West's researches inform us that, in 1983:

...all traces of the ground, and of the Antelope Hotel which gave it its name, have gone, but the inn once stood on the site now covered by the massive Southern Gas building in St Mary's Road, whilst the ground lay across the street, occupying an area of roughly 5 acres bounded to the north by the South Hants Hospital and Brinton's Terrace, to the east by Exmoor Road, and to the south by Oxford Avenue.

Robert West tells us that Daniel Day's tenure at the Antelope was quite brief, moving in 1846 across the river to the Woolston Hotel. The Antelope Hotel became associated with the name of its later landlord, Mr Brooks, who had two daughters, also much connected with the Antelope Ground, one of the most important cricket venues in Hampshire at the time.

Conditioned possibly by demands of harvesting and other work, Hampshire's cricket during the 1840s often continued well into the Autumn. Nearing mid-October 1841 at Cadnam, the Wade and Manor Court Farms XI met Nursling. Into the 1840's Hampshire was developing a number of genuinely strong club sides. Parishes for their part often combined forces to muster a sufficiently viable XI. In June 1841 the parishes of Hinton, Cheriton and Bramdean united to meet

Droxford 'with Stoneage as given mate'. The following season Woodley, Anfield (*sic*), Braishfield and Baddesley combined to play Romsey on Baddesley common. Also in 1842, more than two thousand gathered at Day's Ground to watch Hampshire (67 and 27) lose to All England (99; without 'A Mynn Esq' who was 'busy hopping') followed by a single-innings match. Cricket in July 1842 gained a *Punch* mention.

Hampshire's two County matches with Nottinghamshire in 1843 were marked by incident. For the away fixture at Trent Bridge, Hampshire arrived three men short, and were obliged to recruit Thomas Chamberlayne's footman plus two Nottingham locals, and then suffered an innings defeat. When Nottinghamshire were en route to the return at Southampton, disaster befell their player Thomas Barker. The *Hampshire Advertiser* in July 1843 reported: 'Barker, the bowler, on leaving Lords for the Southampton Railway on the Wednesday to play for Nottingham, was ran away with in a local cab, jumped out and sustained a severe fracture of the leg.' Hampshire allowed Francis Noyes to bat twice in each innings for Nottinghamshire, with Noyes making 31 and 8, then 5 and 9 in his side's 39 runs win. Included in the Nottingham XI were William Clarke, later of All England fame, taker of 476 wickets in all cricket during 1855, with Samuel Redgate, 11 wickets in the match and described elsewhere as 'very fast and ripping'.

Also unusual during 1843 were the tactics of East Meon in a fixture that saw opponents Fareham level on runs with 3 wickets to fall. A press report tells that:

At this period the whole of the eleven in the field, with the exception of the bowler, was placed behind the hitter's wicket, and the ball put up with speed from the powerful hand of Etherington. The effect of this novel arrangement was decisive, and prevented the loss of the game to the East Meon party. Each scored 92.

The remarkable 'Felix' (Nicholas Wanostrocht), cricketer, inventor, writer and artist, made an intriguing impact on the 1844 Hampshire cricket scene. Felix had around 1837 invented a bowling machine, 'The Catapulta', capable of delivering a ball of controlled pace and pitch at the batsman's wicket. Felix stated that the device could in its original form, be traced back to Roman times. It was used in a game played in late season 1844 at Day's Ground. The Gentlemen took on the Players of the South Hants Club and ten Catapulta wickets in all were taken on behalf of the Gentlemen. The *Hampshire Independent* wrote of it being 'the first match in our locality in which that splendid bowling machine has been used.' Catapulta also featured at Tichborne Down and George Smith 'created some amusement by running half way over to meet the ball' before it touched the ground, at which 'the Catapult was stealthily altered by Mr Chamberlayne to meet the dodge, and the next ball took the wicket.'

Thomas Chamberlayne became M.C.C. President for 1845, and became Hampshire's President in 1863, at the re-forming of the County Cricket Club. A man of varied interests, he had contributed much to cricket in Hampshire.

At club level, team professionals during the 1840s might expect to receive a benefit of some kind, often a match played for the purpose. The Isle of Wight granted their player Tinley such a match in 1846, where a sixpence admission fee had the effect of 'keeping the company in the field reasonably select'.

The later 1840s saw a number of innovations, among them provision of telegraph score boards and the printing of score cards. Of the Hampshire versus All England match advertised for late June 1849 it was stated that : 'J. and F. Lillywhite will be in attendance on the Ground with a Printing Press to give the scores.' A closely fought encounter at Day's Woolston Ground brought a *Hampshire Advertiser* comment that 'Never was a game more strenuously contested by both parties.' Hampshire's Fourteen made 74 and 83 (F. Compton 24 not out), with All England's 83 (Parr 32 not out) and 75 for 8 taking them to a win by 2 wickets. Hillyer and Clarke bowled unchanged for All England, as did Bathhurst and Day for the County. In dismissing England's Lindow, Sir Frederick Bathhurst 'gave him such a switcher that he was fain to substitute his leg for the bat, and the penalty was O.U.T.'

Among the 1800 or so spectators at the first day of the All England XI game was, according to press reports, a man of 103 years of age, reputed to have 'witnessed nearly every match played' in the town for the last ninety years. Daniel Day is said to have brought the old gentleman along, thinking to raise a few shillings for him, only for Day's attentions to be required by demands of the cricket.

Of other 1849 interest, Dorset visited Southampton's Antelope Ground to make 103 and 84 against 154 (Day 67) and 34 for 5 against South Hants. Dorset reversed matters at Weymouth a short while later, scoring 58 and 86 to the 59 and 50 of South Hants. In the north of Hampshire, hundreds of spectators were at 'the sequestered village of Long Sutton' to see the Merry Maids defeat the Matrons. Also to the north, Bramshill (with Day) enjoyed a 101 runs victory over the visiting I. Zingari, whose founders 'were so busy in making history that they had little time to record it'.

Rains of July 1849 replenished the turf of Brook's Antelope Ground at Southampton to restore 'in a considerable degree its carpet-like surface'. At Ryde, the home side's win over Ventnor was followed by an excellent dinner then farewells to the 'Ventnorians' amidst 'the cheers of the victor, and the pityless pelting rain'. In a summer more inviting that its predecessor, cricketers in the Woodley Park grounds of W. Stead Esq., prolonged the season well into October 1849 with a single-wicket match.

4

Becoming a Sport

CRICKET WAS BY 1850, Christopher Brookes wrote in *English Cricket: The Game and Its Players Through the Ages,* on the road from 'being little more than an aristocratic diversion' to 'well on the way to becoming a sport, an occupation and a career'.

Certainly in Hampshire the game was developing on many fronts. Already the shape of cricket throughout village, school, club, Services and county representative teams could be seen. The second half of the century, although again with spells of waning interest, would show, overall, major steps forward.

A comfortable All England victory over Hampshire's Fourteen at Itchen during 1850 led to the County increasing its numbers to twenty, achieving a draw much through the efforts of Bathhurst and Day with 18 wickets between them in the match. Less well received was an 1850 occasion at Ringwood, which drew comment:

> FEMALE CRICKETERS. Eleven women of Lyndhurst and Minstead played other eleven of Poulner and Picket Post, on Thursday, when the latter were victorious. The scene was a disgusting one and altogether discreditable to the district.

The idea of women enjoying themselves at sport was still some way from the mind of that particular reporter, albeit there was now within Hampshire a precedent for such an event.

A cricketing landmark in 1851 was the publication of the Revd James Pycroft's *The Cricket Field.* Travelling long journeys and talking with celebrated cricketers, James Pycroft was able to open up all kinds of avenues into the past through his writing. We are able to read of William Beldham's recollections, widely discussed for their relevance to the formation years of Hambledon cricket. The Revd Pycroft tells of scorers with 'large tin telegraphic letters above their heads' of Mr E.H. Budd's bat weighing 'nearly three pounds' and Mr Ward's a pound more; of Freemantle's famous hit '130 yards in the air'.

In early October 1851 at Itchen, Hampshire's Twenty achieved a draw with an All England XI that included Felix, John Wisden and Julius Caesar. England scored 93 and 72, Hampshire 41 and 33 for 12. In the County's first innings, 13 of the Hampshire batsmen failed to score, the last 8 wickets 'fell for nothing'.

A number of public houses in Hampshire have carried, through the years, names of cricketing connection. Henry Misselbrook, a native of Otterbourne and keeper of The Cricketers' Arms there, in addition to his services to South Hants and appearance for Hampshire, had several Oxford engagements as a bowler.

After the Winchester Assizes of 1851, the learned Judge Coleridge, 'having disposed of all the cases', presided over a cricket match between the North Hants Bar and that of the Western Circuit, the West winning by 145 to 127. 'Aesop' wrote of the occasion:

> Several motions were made with great beauty and manliness, but the merits and not the technicalities were attended to. His lordship appeared to be quite as much pleased as if the matter had been a lively argument upon a special demurrer.

Following its separation from Clarke's All England XI, the United All England XI in 1852 met Twenty Gentlemen of Hampshire, with Day, at Portsmouth, where the County achieved a draw. Entertaining Middlesex at Tichborne Down, Hampshire lost a low scoring encounter by 81 and 45 to 36 and 63. The period around 1852 saw cricket played in meadows later to become the site of Bournemouth's Upper Pleasure Gardens. In an Enham meadow of 1852, Enham Village held Andover well before going down by 2 wickets. A century from T. Adams contributed in large measure in 1852 to Bramshill's convincing success over East Hants.

During an 1853 summer of 'long-continued wet weather', Thomas Dixon introduced a cane-handled bat. A rubber insertion later reduced jarring, with a rubber-handled grip to follow in 1880, when a top-quality bat would cost 21 s. and a ball up to 7s. 6d. Hampshire's twenty-two men in opposition to the United England XI during late September 1853 were defeated by 70 and 42 to 62 and 34. In the County's second innings the last 9 wickets went without score, part of Hampshire's claim to 22 noughts from 44 individual innings.

Apart from continued reports during 1854 of established teams such as South Hants, Winchester College and Bramshill, there was mention of clubs being formed in places like Oakley Park and Highclere. Cricket reporting around this time suggested social distinctions between players within the game: 'Bodle' for instance, 'John Lillywhite' and 'E. Moore Esq.' not everyone was accorded the title Esquire!

Hampshire's military presence during 1855 was reflected in teams such as Winchester Garrison, Parkhurst Barracks, Hampshire Militia and the Royal Marines Artillery taking the field. Of civilian clubs, among those mentioned are Crawley, King's Somborne, Petersfield School, Portsmouth Borough and

Alresford. East Hants C.C. engaged Charles Arnold of Cambridge as its professional bowler for the season. *Scores and Biographies* described Charles Arnold as of 'tremendous' pace, 'delivering many shooting balls, which have proved very fatal and destructive.' Enlistment of professional players by Hampshire's major clubs is a measure of the seriousness with which the matter of winning matches was approached. Score sheets of the time give a marked indication of the effect that such a cricketer could have on a game.

In September 1855 the first known match at the Folly, Basingstoke (later to be known as May's Bounty) saw Newbury defeat Basingstoke by 17 runs. Put to a different purpose was the Antelope Ground, where the children of Southampton's Ragged School were entertained with a variety of games and 'a bountiful supply of cakes and tea'.

The weather of 1855 offered variety in the extreme. A long-sustained late summer at Winchester contrasted sharply with an Isle of Wight thunderstorm that left scarcely a Newport upper window unbroken, plus tiles and slates broken by lumps of ice.

May 1856 welcomed the ending of war celebrations, with a Sunday Thanksgiving Day for the Restoration of Peace. Although rain affected some of the limited cricket played in Hampshire during 1856 (John May indicates nothing of record for the County in *Scores and Biographies*), there was August heat producing temperatures of up to 88 degrees in the shade.

Reports from 1856 highlight a number of notable individual and team performances. For All Muggleton v. Oakley Park, Colonel Smith scored nought and 113. Henry Frere took 12 wickets in all for Basingstoke against the Isle of Wight. Emmett captured 9 first-innings wickets for West Meon and neighbourhood Farmers (who included an Arnold and a Hammond in their ranks), but was still in a side defeated by 47 and 44 to 8 and 42. There was, though, the consolation of an excellent dinner provided on the ground by Mr Lewis of the Red Lion Inn. Hampshire provided a further M.C.C. president in 1857, when Sir F.H. Hervey-Bathurst was nominated for office.

There were outstanding individuals who attracted praise. Luff of Twyford bowled 'left handed under trolling' from which few players could 'make a long score'. There are a number of names that recur frequently in Hampshire cricket. In addition to that of Luff we find regular mention of Arnold, Tate, Compton, Butler, Morant, Crouch, Budd, Read, Hill, Totterdale, Adams, and White.

In addition to published scores, match reports grew more frequent during the 1850s. Compliments were often generous: Hyde House School was in 1859 applauded for 'exquisite fielding' against South Western C.C. at Winchester's Roebuck Ground. Criticism was sometimes sharp. Of the three wickets in hand by which South Hants beat South Wilts in 1857, it was written that they were 'not worth a run each'. The Isle of Wight Cricket Club proclaimed that 'we never trouble reporters with the scores of our matches'. Happily for posterity, there are ample Island reports to provide a rich account of cricket there. As a sombre thought at a time of fine hot summer, the *Isle of Wight Gazette* in June 1858 considered that 'Foreign affairs have an ugly look'.

The spring of 1860 brought reports of Rifle Corps being formed in various parts of Hampshire. A Rifle Brigade team from Aldershot lost to I. Zingari at Lord's in September 1860. The early 1860s were marked by appearances of strong All England XIs in various parts of the county. Provision of match bowling analyses, together with end-of-season averages provided cricket followers with ample statistical interest. One-day fixtures, often enabling each team to bat twice in its entirety, gave bowlers ample opportunity to make and sustain a reputation.

The summer's weather of 1861, described as of 'gloom, then bright hope' had qualities similar to the fortunes of cricket. Joy certainly at Southsea during August 1861 where Twenty-two of East Hants Club and Ground with 152 and 112 defeated the United Eleven of England (126 and 94) before a crowd of over twenty thousand. At Sherborne St John, the Vyne with 151 (D. Chute 50) beat Tangier Park 82 (E. Wither 55 not out, having taken 6 wickets in the Vyne innings, R. Wither taking the other 4) and 56. Occupying the remaining time the Vyne made 66 and Tangier Park 48 for 7. Tangier Park won the return, with 67 more runs from E. Wither, as well as 9 wickets in the Vyne's second innings, plus a stumping from the bowling of W. Chandler. Also enjoying marked success with the ball during the 1860s was New Forest's professional David Ruffell.

Late season 1863 was important for the formation of a revived County Cricket Club for Hampshire. A meeting was held in August 1863, with a further gathering at Southampton on 11 September. Thomas Chamberlayne became club president with George Matthew Ede (a well-known amateur jockey, dying from injuries in the Grand National of 1870) as honorary secretary. Mr J. Hunt became hon. treasurer, with the support of an elected committee. The Antelope Ground at Southampton was the club headquarters. One hundred and forty members enrolled at 1 guinea a head, a marquee was bought, a club standard ordered, and fixtures arranged for the coming year.

Apart from activities of the revitalized Hampshire County Cricket Club, 1864 saw other landmarks, including legalization of 'overhand bowling' and the first issue of John Wisden's *Cricketers' Almanack*. Of absorbing interest to Hampshire cricket followers was the late September 1864 announcement of the forthcoming Sporting Reminiscences of Hampshire by 'Aesop'. While a number of clubs within the county met setbacks during 1864, including Ringwood 'apparently deserted by those who constitute its members', Southampton Drapers and Grocers showed no lack of enthusiasm. It was reported of them:

Our friends 'the dewbeaters' have just sprung into new life and activity, and established a promising club under the title of 'the Alexandra'. They practice in the park every morning from 5 to 7 o'clock and awaken the slumbers around with their merry shouts.

Many working people at this time had limited free time during the day, and such early starts were not unusual in parts of Hampshire.

Revival of interest around 1865 was evident in a number of ways. The stronger clubs made use of established professionals, with James Southerton in the Southampton area and a photographed 'Mr Cutts, professional Cricketer, Lymington' among those to the fore. The county press featured bowling analyses, although in its end-of-season summary in 1865 Southampton Union C.C. regretted that the figures 'had not been so perfectly taken as to render it possible to publish a correct statement of the averages'. The Union was, however, able to record a tenth wicket stand of 115 between G.R. Nunn and M. Batchelor. Social niceties were not overlooked, certainly not for those involved in the annual Publicans v. Sinners meeting at Mr W.B. Mew's Polars Farm where with the thermometer 'almost up to the boiling point', 'a plentiful supply of moisture' was to hand.

Among newly formed clubs to find mention during 1865 were Pylewell Park, Woolston, Fawley Juveniles, Basingstoke, and Avon Valley (with the Earl Nelson as President). Formation of a village team at Marchwood brought a reminder of basic needs, the *Hampshire Independent* reporting in May 1865: 'it is satisfactory to find the three principle requirements will not be wanting, *viz*, the men, the place and the funds.' Funding was important, with a small club likely to cost around £35 a year to finance. An item of expense coming to notice around 1865 was that of whitewash for the marking of creases.

The 1860s were notable for marked variations in cricket weather. While July 1868 brought reports of a hot, dry, season of a kind not known in southern England for seventy years, with no trace of dew at night, umpires at the M.C.C. v. Surrey match at the Oval a year later were obliged to wear greatcoats against the cold.

High scores, both team and individual, continued to increase. C.F. Lucas in 1866 recorded Hampshire's initial century at first-class level, while Mr H. Gale made 176 of the 405 the Veteran Gentlemen of Hampshire scored against Sussex Veterans. To mark a decisive 79 against Basingstoke in 1867, the Alton Committee presented Arthur Wood with a bat. Dispensing with the use of bats were members of the South-Western and Mid-Hants Broomsticks XI in an 1866 end-of-season Monday fixture 'for the benefit of W. Collins'. Broomsticks made 18 and 35, the Bats 13 and 26. 'The above game terminating early, the parties proceeded to play the return match.' Again over 2 innings per side, Broomsticks were successful. Most batsmen managed at least a run or two during the day, though Misselbrook of Broomsticks seems to have been 'absent 0' on each of his four opportunities to bat.

33

At least those scores from 1866 have been preserved, whereas those for Downton against Fordingbridge remained unavailable, with press hints that the figures had been withheld 'to suppress publication' for whatever reason. While in some places enthusiasm remained for early starts (Timber v. Leather at Yarmouth in the Isle of Wight beginning at 4 a.m. on an August Thursday in 1866) Fareham's 1867 visit to Mid Hants found them late in arriving and four players short, having batting order places listed as 'Emergency'. Something of the country scene of the time was perhaps captured in the annual visit in 1867 by Southampton Clarence C.C. to Cadland Park, where play was 'most pleasant, agreeable and well contested', watched by a gathering that included Lady Elizabeth Drummond and the Bishop of Montreal.

Hampshire's cricket of 1868 was memorably enlivened by a visit of the Australian Aboriginals. Led by Middlesex-born Charles Lawrence, in an England tour extending from May to October, the Aboriginals earned public acclaim not only for colourful cricket, but for remarkable demonstrations of native skills given after the close of cricket play.

Events in Europe occupied much press attention during the 1870s, while at home a number of Army XIs met civilian clubs at cricket. Ice during May 1870 was followed by months of Hampshire drought severe enough to ensure a welcome for August rain. Cricketers at Northwood, Isle of Wight, interrupted a July 1870 match to jump over a hedge and help put out a rick fire. Elsewhere in Hampshire, an XI from Messrs Raynbird, Caldecott and Co. met the Basingstoke Volunteer Fire Brigade.

Excitement prevailed also at Meads, Winchester, where the College's last pair, J.B. Moyle and H. Awdry, having secured a 1 wicket win over Eton, were 'collared by Mr Moore-Stevens, an enthusiastic and glorious old Wykhamist, who gave each boy a five pound note.' Money also featured in the Gentlemen of West Hants fixture at Danebury in late season 1870, where a bet of 2000 to 200 guineas was laid that W.G. Grace 'did not in either of his innings obtain 280 runs'. In the event W.G. Grace's second-innings 65 was instrumental in Danebury's 8 wickets win, and presumably to somebody's advantage in the bet.

Club and village batsmen, as well as those at higher level, must have welcomed the introduction in the 1870s of the heavy roller, a feature to play a major part in the improvement of playing pitches, offsetting the frequently dangerous consequences of underprepared surfaces.

Deanery Cricket Club was formed at Southampton during 1871, thanks greatly to the Revd A.B.O. Wilberforce. In a first version published in 1921, with a later supplementary volume, former Deanery Hon. Secretary Mr F.J. Montgomery tells, in considerable detail and much warm colour, the story of this major club. Along the coast, Charles H. Mate and Charles Riddle describe in *Bournemouth 1810-1910* how during spring 1871 Bournemouth C.C. played against the artillery officers stationed at Christchurch.

Wet weather has throughout the years caused endless grief to cricketers and cricket followers alike, enough to strike a chord in the 1872 description of a Fawley stormy day visit to Cowes when, according to a report, 'the very flags in the field, as if protesting against such inclement weather, bowed their heads and lay prostrate on the ground.'

Acknowledging the areas of doubt concerning any agreed date for the start of cricket's County Championship, Roy Webber in *The County Cricket Championship* regards 1873 as a generally accepted starting point. League and other competitions would come and go throughout Hampshire until taking firm hold during the 1970s and 1980s. In September 1874, however, there was an admission in the *Hampshire Advertiser* that 'Cricket is now at a low ebb in the county, but through the generosity of Lord Londesborough a new life will be imparted to it.' Certainly the game at Lyndhurst and elsewhere benefited much from the patronage of Lord Londesborough. Apart from interest created by the 1878 Australian visit to England, Hampshire reports of various club Annual General Meetings and celebration dinners suggested that cricket was stirring once more. Weather had the decade's last word, with 1879 described as a 'nightmare year of heavy rain'. The 1880s saw something of a rebirth for Hampshire County Cricket Club, with Russell Bencraft at the early stages of a remarkable period of service as player, administrator and guiding force. The club game revived also in many parts of the county. Cadnam Cricket Club was founded in 1880, playing its early matches at Lamb's Corner and from the beginning including names such as Purkiss, Dunning, Henbest, Grayer, Farmers and Bradford. On the saddest on notes, George Frederick Grace, brother of W.G., died in 1880 whilst staying the Red Lion Hotel, Basingstoke. Not yet thirty years of age G.F. Grace had not been well. Able to travel from Downend to Basingstoke, he became confined to the hotel by an inflammation of the lungs, from which he died, not long after having played for England against Australia.

The season of 1882 saw a number of Hampshire cricketing landmarks. Dean Park, Bournemouth, staged the County's game with Somerset, while at Portsmouth's United Services Ground, Cambridge Past and Present met the touring Australians. The United Services venue was also the scene of 386 runs from J. Spens against Nondescripts. Francis Lacey who would during 1887 score 323 not out for Hampshire against Norfolk and in later years become a noted secretary to the M.C.C., in 1882 averaged more that a hundred with the bat.

At a time when wickets were said to have been improving, Surrey in 1883 made 650 versus Hampshire at the Oval. J. Martin of Stockbridge played a remarkable part in that club's 10 wickets win over Abbott's Ann, 'accomplishing the unprecedented feat of taking the whole of the 20 wickets with an average of 2 runs per wicket.' Also during 1883, for the newly formed Boldre C.C. v. Beaulieu Rails, W. Pratt made 102 of Boldre's 259 runs, then in the opposition dismissals for 38 and 74 took 9 wickets plus a stumping. In the Portsmouth area during

1883 and succeeding seasons, Doctor Arthur Conan Doyle, later to use cricketers' names in some of his celebrated Sherlock Holmes and other stories, was not only making a cricket mark as an all-rounder under his own name, but also as the strong Portsmouth full-back or goalkeeper 'A.C. Smith'.

A revised Code of the Laws of Cricket was adopted by the M.C.C. during 1884. Owing much to William Pickford and other sportsmen of the Bournemouth district,the South Hants and Dorset Football association was formed during 1884, to be succeeded in 1887 by separate Dorset County and Hampshire Football Associations. Hampshire links between football and cricket clubs have in the past been particularly strong with, as in the Football League, a number of soccer clubs coming into being from cricket origins.

Hampshire cricket in 1884 continued to expand in a number of directions. South Hants C.C.'s 1884 West Country travels included Glastonbury, Taunton and Yatton. The visiting Philadelphians concluded their 1884 tour of England as guests of Admiral Hornby and Portsmouth port officers at a dinner on board the *Victory* to commemorate the anniversary of the Battle of the Nile. Along the coast, A.E. Stoddart, to achieve fame as an English cricketer and rugby footballer, showed young promise with two centuries for Bournemouth.

Among clubs particularly active in 1884, Ordnance Survey played 30 out of 34 planned fixtures, with Major F. Fellowes, R.E., taking 84 wickets at 7.81 runs each. Totton Juniors staged a brave 1884 recovery. Having registered 10 'duck's eggs' in their first innings of 10 runs in reply to Bartley Seniors' 42, Totton then dismissed their opponents for 30 before achieving a 4 wickets win. Mindful of the needs of others, Southampton in September 1884 staged cricket and supporting events in aid of the Distressed Cricketers' Fund.

Press comments around 1885 told not only of cricket clubs being formed (Corhampton, Wellow Park, St Andrew's Juniors) and those short of required officers (Nursling), but also of various events (Hythe and Dibden C.C. - a concert) needed to bring in the required income. Reports from club A.G.M.s emphasized their need for fund-raising. During 1885 the new County Ground at Bannister Road, Southampton was first used. Publication that year of *The Hampshire Cricketers Guide* was a welcome contribution to the scene.

While the Green Jackets' 1885 Cricket Week at St Cross attracted interest at home, the Hampshire Regiment abroad also made cricket news, with high totals including 597 at Floriana, Malta against 289 from the Royal Artillery. For winter 1885 pursuit *The New Indoor Game - Cricket* was available for 1s. 1/2d. post free.

Towards the later 1880s, cup competitions gained an increasing hold on Hampshire cricket, bringing together teams of considerable strength. While the major clubs could sustain fixture lists of thirty or more games a season, enlivened by cup spice, others settled for around a dozen or so matches, with annual subscriptions of about 7s. 6d. The Challenge Cup Competition of 1888 brought runs (Portsmouth 435, Havant 119) and rewards (Ringwood presented a cane-handled bat with inscribed silver plate to Mr A.C. Holmes for 115 not out against Romsey).

Southampton Public Parks Cricket Association had its formation in 1889, with Mr Tankerville Chamberlayne presenting a challenge cup with base made of wood from his yacht *Arrow* and silver bands on which the name of each year's winner could be inscribed. Some fifty years later, in 1941, eighty-four-year-old Mr Harry Weeks recalled for the *Southern Daily Echo* his recollections of Parks' matches of 1889 and after. Mr Weeks remembered Maurice Read of Surrey playing for Waltham Green; P. Crimmins, 100 wickets in a Parks' season and on one occasion 5 wickets in successive deliveries; the outstanding ability of Ralph Ruffell, Southampton Park cricketer and former 'Saints' goalkeeper; impressive hitters such as Captain Wynyard (noted figure skater and in the Old Carthusians forward line at the 1881 F.A. Cup Final). With good cause also to remember 1889, Holy Trinity in the Southampton Schools competition dismissed St Mark's for nought, 6 wickets to Pointer.

Having overcome the problems of a wet summer in 1890, Hampshire clubs welcomed the improved weather of 1891, but had to consider the need to improve facilities, weighed against the need to remain financially afloat. While economics led to the amalgamation of some clubs, others were able to develop and expand.

Press reports of 1891 included the names of clubs both old and relatively new, among them Bishop's Waltham, Bartley, Andover, Hythe Choir, Corhampton, Geneva Cross, Sopley, H.M.S. *Invincible*, Handel College, Romsey Lodge Buffaloes.

Winchester won the County Cricket Cup competition in 1892 for the third successive season: Deanery 166 and 280 (Pink taking 13 wickets in all), Winchester 349 and 98 for 8. Of individual achievement, Portsmouth-born seventeen-year-old Ernest Read, later to appear for both Hampshire and Sussex, in 1892 for South Hants v. Adelaide, made 30 (including a seven) in six scoring shots, and then took 8 for 27 in his team's victory.

One of the sunniest summers within memory encouraged fast wickets and high scoring during 1893. The Australians at Portsmouth United Services Ground, 'as firm and true as the proverbial billiard ball' totalled 843 but were unable to force a win against Oxford and Cambridge Past and Present. Hampshire met some difficulty in team raising during 1893, prompting 'Hawkeye' to write in the *Hampshire Independent* that 'one cannot help suspecting that the honour of the old county is a consideration second to that of personal convenience'. At club level there were certainly players of ability. Stubbington House School opener Darcy Lever was an all-rounder of marked achievement. Russell Bencraft's century for Hampshire Hogs against Major Maud's XI just failed to avert a 1 run defeat. Three seasons earlier Russell Bencraft made an unbeaten 243, and is on record as having scored a century on each day of the week when a student at St George's Hospital. Apart from his prowess with the bat, few men in Hampshire cricket have given more in such a variety of directions as Russell Bencraft, knighted later in life and from 1936 to his death president of the County Cricket Club.

Hampshire in 1894 received the South Africans at Southampton, when wet weather prevented a result. The following season Hampshire were competing in the fourteen-team County Championship, taking tenth place by virtue of six wins against nine defeats. Vic Issacs, Hampshire's scorer and statistician of the 1970s and 1980s has, among his many valuable undertakings, provided in typescript form a readily useable summary of Hampshire's match scores from that 1895 date.

League competition was much in the minds of Hampshire's cricket administrators towards the end of the nineteenth century. Early in 1896 a meeting was convened at Scullard's Hotel, Southampton, with a view to forming a league that would, it was hoped, include Deanery, Romsey, Ordnance Survey, Southampton and Trojans. A Bournemouth and District League operated from 1897, with Boscombe the inaugural winners, followed by Christchurch (1898), and Kinson during 1899. The winter of 1896/97 saw the formation of a Hampshire Football League, with teams from Cowes, Freemantle, Southampton, Eastleigh, Bournemouth, Andover, Ryde and Royal Artillery.

Prominent for Deanery around 1898 was Victor Barton, Netley-born and appearing for Kent from 1889 as 'Bombadier Barton'. Joining Hampshire in 1895 Victor Barton proved an all-rounder good enough to win an England cap and as a striker of the ball, powerful enough to produce in fieldsmen a 'wholesome dread of him'.

The improved weather of 1899 enabled Hampshire cricket to see the century out in positive fashion. While the county side ended 1899 ordinarily enough, sharing tenth championship place with Notts, there was now a Hampshire 2nd XI which would in time open up opportunities for younger players throughout. Major club sides would now undertake a programme of thirty or more matches. Village teams, restricted often by the demands of work and the limitations of daylight, might settle for fifteen or so. While some of the leading clubs engaged professionals or used players with county backgrounds, there was also an extension of coaching. 'In the interests of Hampshire cricket' Mr C.A.R. Hoare of Hamble engaged the Nottinghamshire and England cricketer, Alfred Shaw, to coach on a matting wicket at Hamble until the end of April 1899. Club secretaries were invited to send selected players for coaching by Alfred Shaw, named by Richard Daft as 'The Emperor of Bowlers' who took over 2000 wickets in his career at around a dozen runs apiece.

Victor Trumper, named 'immortal' in Jack Fingleton's biography of him, would have had many recollections of a successful 1899 Australian tour of England, some of the most memorable events occurring off the field of play. During the tourists' drawn game at Southampton during August 1899, in which he was not playing, Victor Trumper, with Australian colleagues Frank Laver and Alfred Johns, was taken to the Royal Squadron Yacht Club at Cowes, where Trumper was introduced to the Prince of Wales (the future King Edward VII). While strolling on the lawn, the cricketers encountered a horse-drawn carriage bearing Queen Victoria. Peter Sharpham's biography of Victor Trumper tells that 'As Victor and his team-mates bowed their heads the elderly monarch returned the greeting.' Earlier in 1899, the Revd C.G. Lane, vicar of Portsea, former Oxford University and Surrey cricketer, had preached before the Queen at Osborne on the Island and was at the Queen's dinner party.

Also with thought of cricket and hospitality during 1899 was Fred Major of Fawley, who in a diary made available through Graham Bowen wrote: 'Nov. 14th Cricket supper at Falcon Inn, A.C. Drummond in the chair it went off a treat the best we ever had, W. Davy Bat, G. Gardner a bat, J. Mintram a ball, W. Major a ball, J. Adams 2/6d from Mr Garner.'

5

The Twentieth Century

THE TWENTIETH CENTURY opened in Hampshire with a season of mainly fine cricket weather, not until the end of August 1900 did Southampton Parks League experience any rain interruption. As an early omen, 'Brusher' Mills, the noted New Forest snake-catcher and brusher of Lyndhurst's Bolton's Bench wicket, captured three adders in March 1900, regarded as 'very early'.

The county press was generous in space allotted to match reports, showing a number of clubs making use of paid professionals, Sam Hooton and Smoker prominently so. Cricketers with first-class experience also made a mark on Hampshire club cricket into the 1900s, the Revd A.L. Porter, E.M.C. Ede, W.M. Turner (Essex), Christopher Heseltine (later to become Hampshire's president), Lieutenant C.H. Abercrombie, and E.B. Shine of University match fame (1896), among them.

The laws continued to be subject to variations here and there. The over was in 1900 fixed at six balls, subject to certain alterations in wartime and other circumstances. Proposals to add a fourth stump were not pursued. Although Hampshire used ten bowlers in their 1900 encounter with Yorkshire at Hull, there were those in the Bournemouth area, notably fifteen-year-old C. Brown, Bournemouth's professional, Head, and Hooper of Temperance C.C., who found three stumps plenty to aim at.

The summer of 1901 was conducive to run scoring (C.B. Fry six consecutive first-class centuries), batting information was plentiful and club reporting colourful, however there was a tendency to omit bowling analyses. At a time when the county side cost around £12 000 a season to run, the club game was much indebted to supporters such as Mr Edward l'Anson for instituting in the Grayshott area (in 1901) a cup competition that provided welcome impetus. In the south of the county, Hinton Admiral's 1901 Cricket Week, through the encouragement of Sir George Meyrick, attracted teams such as Free Foresters, Aldershot Division and I. Zingari (for whom C.S. Marriott took 9 for 45) to that part of Hampshire. While the County XI's 1901 improvement (from bottom to half way) owed much to the bowling of C.B. Llewellyn and the batting of Captain J.G. Greig, there was also encouragement for the future with the formation of a number of boys' teams.

A wet summer of 1902 saw Hampshire once more at the bottom of the County Championship, with a percentage of minus 66.66 from sixteen matches. Hampshire's summer of 1903 proved even wetter than the previous year. Dean Park staged a Gentlemen v. Players match in which W.G. Grace appeared, although to no great effect. Conscious, as with the game at all levels, of the need to explore every kind of fund-raising avenue, the County Cricket Club arranged a production of *Caste*.

In each of the three seasons from 1904, Hampshire's county side trod new first-class ground. In July 1904, at Alton, Hampshire received and lost to the South Africans who had arrived at Southampton on the Union Castle liner *Saxon* two months earlier. Surrey took the points from their visit to Aldershot of May 1905, while Warwickshire at Basingstoke in 1906 found Hampshire ready to field in heavy rain, enabling Warwickshire to complete their winning bid.

Club scores continued to vary between extremes. At the lower end, Burley in 1905 dismissed Milford for just 2 runs, 5 wickets each for the Revd A.B. Cummins and his brother Bertie. Also during 1905, Brockenhurst made 418 (Smoker 134, A. Clarke 159 not out) to defeat Deanery by an innings and 211 runs at Brockenhurst Park. At Brockenhurst in 1906, Mr E. Morant's ground reflecting much credit on groundsman Smoker, Devon Dumplings totalled 529 (Major Tristram 210, Dr Roache 139) with A. Scott-Murray 'nearly a century and a half' in the home reply of 446. In a further 1906 Brockenhurst Cricket Week run feast, Mr B. Morant's XI made 203 (Hayter 113) and Mr E. Morant's team over 500, brothers F. and A. Scott-Murray gaining the distinction of each making a century in the same innings.

With cup as well as league contest growing throughout the county in the early 1900s, there were moves towards a competition between Hampshire's various cricket leagues. Of intriguing county-level interest, Jack Hobbs, to begin his distinguished Surrey career the following season, during 1904 fielded as a substitute for Hampshire against Surrey, taking an outstanding catch to dismiss the Surrey captain, Lord Dalmeny. Also of Surrey connection, Battersea-born Philip Mead, having been given a Surrey trial as a slow left-handed bowler, became Hampshire qualified in 1906, beginning a career that brought the County 48 892 runs at an average of 48.84, 266 wickets at around 35 runs apiece, and 627 catches at approaching 1 per match.

In defiance of wet weather (almost!), Hampshire clubs in 1907 adopted the practice of playing additional time-limit games if daylight enough remained when the scheduled fixture was completed. Local rivalry remained keen, Beaulieu in 1907 going to some trouble to recruit Hampshire's Alec Kennedy for a needle match, while efforts towards establishing a Hampshire Cricket Leagues Association persisted. Victory tasted as sweet as ever, emphasized in Tony Pawson's *Runs and Catches* quoting Jack Parr's account of the triumphant return from Eton of the 1907 Winchester College cricketers:

When the victorious team returned a vast crowd met them at the station. We processed down through Jewry Street with the town band leading the team. So great was the crush in Kingsgate Street that several people fainted. But the crowd would not disperse for an hour or more and in response to their chanting Pawson addressed them and the hero of the hour, the young Parke, was brought from bed in pyjamas and dressing gown before they would go home.

The Eton and Winchester match was at that time a major event, said to compare in the social calendar with a mini-Ascot. Reminiscence remained very much a part of Hampshire cricket. At Chilbolton C.C.'s Village Hall Supper of November 1907, Mr Andrew Baker spoke from his recollection as a member for more than fifty years.

With doubts in 1908 touching the county game (Dr W.G. Grace in the *Morning Post* recommended a championship of two divisions, eight teams in each, with promotion and relegation a feature), the Hampshire club scene continued to flourish. Recapturing something of the past, Hambledon at Broad-halfpenny Down in 1908 met an All England XI, at which occasion a commemorative granite memorial featured. Over three days, England made 124 (J. Newman 8 for 54) and 309 (G. Leach 80, A.W. Roberts 69, J. Newman 5 for 66), to which the winning Hambledon scores were 277 (Revd W. V. Jephson 114 not out, Captain E.G. Wynyard 59, E.H. Killick 4 for 44) and 158 for 5 (C.B. Fry 84 not out).

Hambledon, in 1907, drew an *Evening Standard* suggestion that a 'Home for Aged Cricketers' should be established, and where better, it was said, than Hambledon.

C.B. Fry's Hampshire debut in 1909, having transferred his allegiance from Sussex, found him top scorer (42 and 60) in each innings against Surrey, but this in an overwhelming defeat in the face of 742 from Surrey. Two years later, C.B. Fry followed 258 not out for Hampshire v. Gloucestershire with a century for the *Mercury* officers and two for the Training Ship *Mercury*.

Having experienced soft wickets and relatively low club scores during 1910, Hampshire cricket suffered many pitches 'hard as iron' in the heat of 1911. All credit to W.J. Bendry of Broughton, a student at Hartley University College, Southampton, who not only reached 100 wickets during the season, but also totalled more than 1000 runs.

Clubs had to be nothing if not enterprising at this time. Simon Rowley's *Burley C.C. Centenary Year Handbook*, 1875-1975, tells how for Burley's 1912 season not only did the club move its pavilion in entirety from one site to another on an adapted timber wagon, but that turf for a ground formerly covered in gorse and containing a pond was transported from Badbury Rings in neighbouring Dorset.

Finance continued to be important. The County Club's balance in 1912 dropped from around £193 to little more than nought. Millbrook C.C. held its own on an income of around £30, of which £24 was made up of subscriptions. The January 1912 edition of C.B. Fry's *Magazine* advocated that county clubs seek enough members to become independent of gate money: 'That is the way of salvation from the danger of mob rule.'

Cricket fortunes, including finance, are to a large extent at the mercy of weather. Abnormal rains in August 1912 flooded many Hampshire roads and almost cut off isolated villages. They may also have been the reason for the delay until October 1912 of the conclusion of the New Forest Boys' Cricket League, won eventually by Boldre Church of England School, F. Jenvey taking 59 wickets for just 111 runs. In the seasons leading up to the First World War of 1914-18, Hampshire cricket was developing in a number of directions. The Hampshire side was holding its own in the County Championship, with Lionel Tennyson and gifted Rugby International C.H. Abercrombie making a striking impact. The *Hampshire County Cricket Guide* continued to be well received, as did the 1913 indication of a series of club and ground matches aimed at the advance of younger players. However, on the Isle of Wight in 1913, six East Cowes lads were convicted of stealing bats, seventeen balls and other cricket items belonging to the Osborne Royal Naval College. One boy was ordered to be birched, the others were bound over.

Hampshire's August Bank Holiday 1913 match with Middlesex drew a Monday attendance of 7500 to Southampton, of whom 6100 paid gate money of £163. At club level, while individual bowlers continued to excel (C. Heath 107 wickets at 3.48 for Alma, winners in 1913 of the Southampton Public Lands League), 1913 was noted for run scoring - totals of 200 and 300 were frequent. The Trojans' 394 for 4 declared (opener H.A.H. Smith, 187) against 218 from Basingstoke gives an indication of such feats. H.A.H. Smith of Trojans would seem to be the Hamilton A.H. Smith who not only appeared for Hampshire twenty-seven times at cricket, but also for his county at rugby and hockey.

6

Wartime 1914 - 1918

ALTHOUGH THE SUMMER OF 1914 was overshadowed by events leading to war between the Allied and Central European Powers, cricket functioned more or less normally for much of the season. The weather was variable, with the Isle of Wight recording several degrees of frost in June.

Away to an early start was the newly formed Calmore Cricket Club, owing much to Mr E A Maton, who provided a field and scoring box as well as preparing match day pitches. On the 13 April 1914, Calmore Married played the Singles, with Miss Everett and Miss M Louch taking part. Also quickly into the 1914 field was a Southampton Public Lands Association XV, dismissed for 107 (Phil Mead 9 for 24) by Hampshire Club and Ground, who made 342 for 7 wickets. Phil Mead had not long arrived back at Southampton on a Union Castle liner, returning from South Africa with the M.C.C. For the M.C.C., Phil Mead had formed a successful left wing partnership with Frank Woolley in a football match win at Cape Town, this in addition to averaging 54 with the bat during the 1913/14 Tests.

Hampshire's Arthur Jaques had a memorable 1914, his swing bowling bringing him 112 championship wickets, and Neville Cardus later said that the 'pioneer of leg theory based on the in swinging new ball was the almost forgotten Jaques of Hampshire'. Also with cause for satisfaction in 1914, William Moorcroft took 7 Northwood wickets for 9 runs for Deanery at Cowes, while Southampton Grammar School Boys after beating the Parents gave vent to 'naturally unalloyed rejoicing'.

With the outbreak of war on 4 August 1914, a number of cricket clubs brought their season to an abrupt close. In the face of some criticism, prompting public comment from the President (Mr J C Moberly) and Chairman (Doctor Russell Bencraft), Hampshire on M.C.C. advice continued its county programme. The *Southampton Pictorial Souvenir* of the war stated that Hampshire's cricketers joined up 'en masse', training with the 5th Hampshire Battalion on Salisbury Plain. Southampton Volunteers did much of their training at the County Cricket Ground. By December 1914, Hampshire had twenty-four County cricketers in the Armed Forces. As a tribute to courage and a grim reminder of the cost of war, the *Hampshire Advertiser* in its 'Roll of Honour' published regular lists of those who had gone out from town and village.

On the 1914 Home Front, in addition to factory work, meetings were held to organize ambulance, nursing and hospital services. Boom defences were set up in the Western Solent and examination vessels anchored off Yarmouth. Gun barrels were installed at Fort Victoria and Hurst Castle, whereas in other places there were arrests of suspected 'spies'. Playing fields were put to the plough in the interests of food production, so that as well as being without cricketers and officials, many clubs were for the war's duration lacking grounds on which to play. A number of Hampshire cricket clubs held A.G.M.s in 1915, and some arranged provisional fixtures. It soon became clear, however, that club cricket, as with the county game, was almost at a standstill. There was appreciable strength of opinion that it would be wrong to devote attention to sport while the country was at war, and much of the limited cricket played in Hampshire was to provide opposition for Services XIs. Among civilian clubs to plan such fixtures were Havant, Portsmouth, Ascension C.C., Lee-on-Solent, Deanery, Marchwood and Millbrook, whose Walter Prowting continued with a captaincy to which he had first been elected some thirty-three years earlier. Of school XIs, Bournemouth Grammar 160 (H.L. Le Roy 84, J. O'Hara 7 for 42) defeated Southampton Grammar 153 (W.W. Beggs 81). In other sports, bowls and golf were able to operate in various parts of the county.

With George Muir acting as secretary to the County Cricket Club during the absence of Francis H. Bacon on war service (he lost his life in 1915) Southampton's ground was placed at the disposal of the military authorities, whose uses included the staging of recruiting events. The County Ground was also the venue for a match in aid of Highfield Red Cross Hospitals, Jesse Hopkins' XI (157 for 3, Phil Mead 112 not out) and Australian A.M.C. (90), only a few of whom were in possession of cricket gear.

Hampshire cricketers serving abroad featured in a number of matches, with Jack Newman, Ernie Remnant and Walter Livsey selected to play for His Excellency's XI v. an All India team at Bombay. At home during October 1915 occurred the death of cricket's legendary Doctor W.G. Grace. Abroad at war, the cost in terms of casualties was grievously high.

With the weather of 1916 offering no great encouragement, apart from Service XIs there was little Hampshire cricket played. The Royal Navy appeared at Bournemouth, and sides such as the Army Ordnance at Southampton. There was no Southampton Parks League, although a number of schools maintained fixtures. For the Navy against the Army, Lieutenant C.B. Fry, R.N.R., made 67, having with him at the crease for a while his son Stephen Fry, himself to be a Hampshire player between 1922 and 1931, and father of future Oxford University, Hampshire and Northamptonshire batsman Charles Anthony Fry.

While there was a widely held belief in 1917 that wartime England should have no time or place for games, there was also support for the view that having given their all to the tasks before them, people would benefit overall from the relaxation that sport could provide. Teams to take the 1917 field included Jesse Hopkins' XI, Millbrook, Ordnance Survey, United Cricket Club, Rest Camp, The R.A.M.C. and Australian Pioneers. In the Southampton County Ground Final of the Artillery Cup, Corporal Leach's match-winning 6 for 36 was followed by being carried 'shoulder high to the pavilion by his exultant comrades'. In a low-scoring annual corporation match, played this time at Milton Asylum Ground (Southampton 75 and 82 for 4, Portsmouth 64), Councillors Gleave and Short took 5 wickets each for Portsmouth, as did Councillors Ryder and Bowyer for the visitors.

During much of the 1917 season the Summer Time Act offered broad daylight until 9 p.m., however the spring drought was followed by generally uncertain weather. On a welcome note of encouragement towards the year's end, the County Cricket Club Annual Report in November 1917 stated that through the generosity of County Ground shareholders and other contributors, the club's bank overdraft had been cleared, leaving a small balance in hand. Of particularly moving poignancy, former Hampshire cricketer Captain Arthur Jaques, killed in action in 1915, had willed £500 to the County Cricket Club for payment of any outstanding debt and towards the re-starting of the club. The 30th Annual Report of the Hampshire Football Association in 1917 spoke of heavy wartime losses among players and members. This statement was true also for cricket, as with all other walks of life.

The season of 1918 saw some stirring of Hampshire cricket. There was the encouragement of a generally fine summer, dry months ending with welcome rain that extended into the wettest September for some twenty years and more. R.A.F. Beaulieu cricketers met Works XIs. Alresford Ladies and the Ladies of Bishop's Waltham had fixtures reported. Southampton and District's War League operated in the Parks, with Harland and Wolff taking the newly awarded A.J. Day Shield. Southampton Corporation defeated their Portsmouth counterparts and Councillor Ryder made 107 runs. In Winchester College's victory over Harrow, Winchester's opener D.R. Jardine was rated 'a most promising young batsman'. Also in scoring form, Major the Hon. L. Tennyson, with the Machine Gun Corps, made 184 in 105 minutes against Wellingborough School. During September 1918 at Dean Park, Bournemouth's first taste of major cricket since 1914, in the presence of a military band, had Major Tennyson leading an XI that defeated Captain Poyntz's team by 260 (J.B. Hobbs 55, Sgt-Major Hardinge of Kent 72) and 52 for 5 against 121 and 167 (Pte Mead 45).

Of other sports, baseball had gained popularity in parts of Hampshire through American and Canadian troops stationed within the county. The local bowling season opened in May. Servicemen, as in other wartime summers, were able to take part in various athletics and other meetings.

November 1918 brought to an end a war so tragically costly in terms of human life and misery. The year closed with reports of a worldwide epidemic of influenza and pneumonia that took lives numbered in millions.

7

Play Resumes

CRICKET IN 1919 HAD not only the problems associated with resumption after a major war, but also a legacy of a worldwide influenza epidemic the effects of which lasted into the spring. Ronald Mason has written of 1919 that it had 'in many ways the appearance of a hastily improvised picnic'. What was elsewhere termed 'a hectic re-instatement of the first-class game' saw county cricket operate with two-day championship fixtures. Hampshire's own resumption took them to Lord's where they fielded and bowled (Alec Kennedy 7 for 202 in 55 overs) while Middlesex topped 600, double centuries each for Hearne and Hendren. Hampshire club cricket made a generally quiet re-start, although W. Major, twenty-five years with Fawley, was quickly into his stride, 8 wickets for 3 runs against Warsash. Lord Forster of Lepe was President of the M.C.C. in 1919.

Benefitting from a fine summer, Hampshire club cricket was able to take further steps towards recovery in 1920. Southampton Parks League was certainly away to an improved start compared with 1919, when moments after Sir Sidney Kimber had bowled a ceremonial resumption ball, heavy rains flooded the ground. Early in the Southampton Public Lands Division One season of 1920, D. Phillips of Docks United took 4 wickets in 4 balls during the dismissal of Northam Conservatives for 6, and made 27 not out of his team's 44 for 6. Mr E.C. White, a Basingstoke committee member from 1865 and associated with the club prior to that, in 1920 became Basingstoke's president, a remarkable span of service in a club noted for similar feats.

In a season of 1921 that enjoyed fine weather from late April through to mid-September, Hampshire clubs continued to progress, although problems of ground accommodation were beginning to grow. The county population (including the Isle of Wight) was now past the million mark, with the demands of development in competition with needs of land required for sport. The Hampshire team of 1921 gained fourteen wins from twenty-eight matches, rising to sixth place, thanks much to all-round contributions from Jack Newman and Alec Kennedy.

Parts of Hampshire during 1921 saw runs in plenty. A Basingstoke District side made 253 for 12 declared (A. Butler 77) to 308 for 7 (Tennyson 169) from

48

Sir Denys Roberts, President of the M.C.C.

St Catherine's Hill, Winchester, the 'Hills' referred to in Robert Mathew's poem 'De Collegio' as the site of playing cricket by scholars at Winchester College about 1647.

i

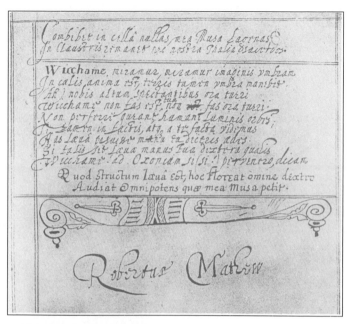

Final lines of Robert Mathew's Latin poem 'De Collegio', written in 1647 while he was a scholar at Winchester College, and believed to be the earliest reference to cricket in Hampshire.

Gentlemen v. Players at Brading, Isle of Wight, c. 1749. From a painting attributed to Francis Hayman.

Thomas Lord, whose name is commemorated in Lord's Cricket Ground, was born at Thirsk, North Yorkshire, in 1755 but died and was buried at West Meon, Hampshire, in 1832.

John Nyren, 1764-1837. Son of Richard Nyren, a major figure in the Hambledon Club and the landlord of the Bat and Ball, John was the author of The Young Cricketer's Tutor *and* The Cricketers of My Time, *published as one volume in 1833.*

iii

The Bat and Ball Inn at Hambledon. Overlooking the cricket ground at Broadhalfpenny, the inn once had as its landlord Richard Nyren, 'the head and right arm' of Hambledon cricket club, according to his son, John.

Cricket at Christchurch Priory, Hampshire, c. 1850.

Dr Henry Maturin was outstanding at club level in the New Forest area, and played for both Middlesex and Hampshire. Later in his career he contributed greatly to the success of Hartley Wintney Cricket Club.

Lyndhurst cricketers outward bound, early 1900s. Cricket has been played at Lyndhurst since 1774, with many notable players, including Reginald Hargreaves, lob bowler for Hampshire between 1875 and 1885. He was married to Alice Liddell, the inspiration for Lewis Carroll's Alice in Wonderland.

v

Sir Russell Bencraft, 1858-1943, was a major figure in Hampshire cricket, achieving distinction as player, captain, secretary and president. He was also a notable rugby player and president of the Hampshire Football Association 1893-5.

The Times, 1 July 1933. Press cuttings, albums and scrap books are an invaluable source of cricket information. Here cups are being exchanged between the captains of Eton and Winchester. Left to right: A.W.E. Winlaw (Captain of Winchester), Sir Oswald Simpkin (Warden of Winchester), Dr James (Provost of Eton), and N.S. Hotchkin (Captain of Eton)

Hampshire County cricketers, Basingstoke, May 1906. Left to right (back row): Jesse Hopkins (groundsman), Alec Bowell, C.B. Llewellyn, Phil Mead, Revd W.V. Jephson, William Langford, Francis Bacon (secretary); (middle row) E. M. C. Ede, John Badcock, E.M. Sprot (captain), Charles Robson; (front row) Capt. J. G. Greig, A.C. Johnston.

Season 1912

The annual general meeting of the Burley Cricket Club was held at the Queens Head on Friday January 12th at 8-30

Present

Rev A B Cummins (Chair)   A E Jackson
A S Eveny   J Robberts   A Y Goddard   A Sims
Y Law   W Marchant   J Marchant   A B Lewis P Lewis

A financial statement was read by the Rev A B Cummins showing a balance of £21 - 17 = 7.

The chairman thought some recognition was due to Mr W P Eveny and Mr E W Tredway for their services as Hon Sec and Hon Treasurer.
On the proposition of Mr J Robberts seconded by Mr A E Jackson it was decided to forward each a vote of thanks for past services

The election of officers for the ensuing season then followed
President Rev W Esdaile   Proposed by Mr A E Jackson
Seconded by W Marchant
Vice Presidents   On the proposition of A Y Goddard
Seconded by W Marchant   To be left to the Secretary

Burley Cricket Club minute book, 1912. Minute books are often the most revealing sources of club cricket information, at times containing the only record of discussion or a decision. Surviving pre-1914 minute books are rare.

John Arnold, Double International. Arnold was an attacking opening batsman and excellent deep fielder for Hampshire from 1929 to 1950, playing for England against New Zealand in 1931. He played on the wing for Southampton and Fulham F. C.s and was picked for England v. Scotland in the 1932-3 season.

Harry Altham played for Oxford University, Surrey and Hampshire. He was a cricket coach at Winchester College for thirty years, an M.C.C. committee member for twenty-five, becoming M.C.C. President in 1959, a President of Hampshire County Cricket Club and a recognized cricket historian.

Autographs of players from a score card of a Gentlemen v. Players match held at Winchester College, 4 September 1943, in aid of Winchester Red Cross Victory Garden Week. Among the autographs are those of Ted Bowley, Alec and Eric Bedser, Ted Drake, Lloyd Budd, Jim Angell, Charlie Knott, Jack Hobbs, Lord Tennyson, Stan Broomfield and Capt. J. P. Gornall.

The Surrey connection. Henry Jupp, an outstanding Surrey and England batsman, who played in the England team in its first ever Test against Australia in 1877. He came to live in Southampton and played as a professional in several Hampshire clubs from around 1883.

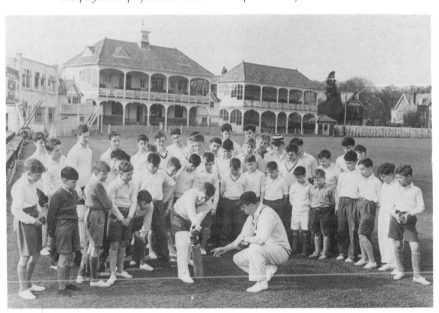

Arthur Holt instructing a class of youngsters at the Southampton County Ground. Among his many sporting achievements (including football for Southampton and cricket for Hampshire), Arthur Holt is best remembered for his qualities as a cricket coach.

Arthur McIntyre, Surrey and England batsman and wicketkeeper, and Surrey coach from 1958. On retiring from county cricket he came to live in Hordle, Hampshire, and gave valued coaching to young Lymington players, of whom David Coles is shown above.

NATIONAL PLAYING FIELDS ASSOCIATION
OFFICIAL SOUVENIR SCORECARD — 6d.

MONDAY, SEPTEMBER 19th, 1949
HAMPSHIRE
VERSUS
H.R.H. THE DUKE OF EDINBURGH'S XI
COUNTY CRICKET GROUND, DEAN PARK, BOURNEMOUTH

HAMPSHIRE

1 McCORKELL, N.				22
2 ROGERS, N. H.				93
3 DAWSON, G.				31
4 BAILEY, J.				16
5 E. D. R. EAGAR (Capt.)				14
6 ARNOLD, J.				30
7 WALKER, C.				13
8 SHACKLETON, D.				7
9 HILL, G.				20
10*HARRISON, L.			Did Not Bat	
11 C. J. KNOTT				

Extras 7

TOTAL 254

Fall of Wickets 1-49 2-150 3-158 4-180 5-181 6-197 7-227 8-254 9-

H.R.H. THE DUKE OF EDINBURGH'S XI

1*S. C. GRIFFITH (Sussex)			6
2 G. O. ALLEN (Middlesex)			27
3 SQUIRES, H. S. (Surrey)			80
4 COMPTON, D. (Middlesex)			52
5 E. R. T. HOLMES (Surrey)			3
6 R. W. V. ROBINS (Middlesex)	not out		35
7 H.R.H. THE DUKE OF EDINBURGH (Capt.)			12
8 F. R. BROWN (Northamptonshire)			18
9 W. S. LOWNDES (Oxford and Hampshire)			11
10 COMPTON, L. (Middlesex)			1
11 GODDARD, T. (Gloucester)			0

Extras 10

TOTAL 255

Fall of Wickets 1-11 2-57 3-131 4-195 5-197 6-206 7-269 8- 9-

Scorer: L. A. Sprankling * Wicketkeeper Umpires: E. Pothecary & F. Chester

Printed and Published by the Hampshire County Cricket Club

Scorecard, Hampshire v. H.R.H. The Duke of Edinburgh's XI, Dean Park, Bournemouth, 19 September 1949.

Ted Bates, Southampton F.C. player, manager and director in turn, and club cricketer with a County trial in 1948. Football commitments prevented this from taking place. His father, William Edric Bates, played cricket for Glamorgan and his grandfather was Yorkshire and England cricketer Billy Bates, whose name is immortalized in verse on the Ashes' urn.

Ted Drake, footballer for Southampton, Arsenal and England, and a member of Hampshire County Cricket Club staff.

Hampshire County cricketers, c. 1954. Left to right (back row): Alan Rayment, Jimmy Gray, Roy Marshall, Derek Shackleton, Reg Dare, Cliff Walker, Leo Harrison; (middle row) Neville Rogers, Charlie Knott, Desmond Eagar (captain), Gerald Hill, Arthur Holt (coach); (front row) Ralph Prouton, Vic Cannings.

Mike Barnard. Much respected as Hampshire cricketer, Portsmouth F.C. footballer, and in recent years as a knowledgeable member of the Radio Solent cricket commentary team.

Lloyd Budd, one of the several former Hampshire County cricketers who later became umpires in the first-class game. Others include: John Arnold, John Holder, Henry Horton and O. W. 'Lofty' Herman, Bob Herman. Lloyd Budd also umpired at Test level.

John Arlott, born in Basingstoke and very much part of Hampshire cricket, about which he has written and broadcast with great warmth.

Umpires successful: 1987. New Forest C.C.A. umpires receive the Southern Area Shield for the fourth successive year. Left to right: Walt Drodge (Chairman of N. F. C. U. A.), John Hardy, Eric Effemey, Bill Carver, Alan Orbell, with Brian Pardey, Chairman of Bashley/Rydal Cricket Club, and himself a former cricketer who has become an umpire.

Geoffrey Ford served Hampshire cricket admirably as a successful cricketer, hon. fixtures secretary and later umpire for Bournemouth Sports Club, becoming well known as chairman of Hampshire County Cricket Club.

Paul Terry, later to play for Hampshire and England, in his club days with Havant, batting against Waterlooville.

Bill Rickman padding-up prior to the innings for Older Elite v. Younger Elite at Pennington in August 1989, at the age of eighty-five.

Former New Forest cricket ground at Bank, near Lyndhurst, 1988. Bank Cricket Club was formed in the 1920s, their ground being leased from the Forestry Commission. Neglected during the Second World War, attempts to revive the pitch were unsuccessful, the club was disbanded and the pitch returned to Forest grazing.

Victor Isaacs (left), Hampshire County Cricket Club's scorer, statistician and public address system announcer, pictured with Worcestershire's scorer, Jim Sewter, in 1988.

Aerial view of Pylewell Park cricket ground, on the edge of the New Forest, in the Pylewell Estate. At the top of the picture is the Solent, with the Isle of Wight beyond.

Ray Pavesi was prominent with bat and ball as Basingstoke & North Hants retained the Echo Trophy in an evening knock-out final at Southampton County Ground in July 1989.

Lawrie Scott at the scoreboard after having made 279 runs in 100 minutes for CLC Charondon against Hendy Ford Mansbridge, in Southampton's Lawson Tools Parks League, August 1989.

Hampshire Over-Fifties, 1989. Left to right (back): Arthur Holt (team manager), Clive Harrison, Ken Langley, Jeremy Peters, John Rickard, Howard Wright-Green, Brian Ferkins, Vic Loveless (chairman); (front) Stan Rudder, Jim Stares, Derek Tulk (captain), Mike Chauffourier, Bernard Harrison.

Forest Final, Bolton's Bench, Lyndhurst, July 1989. Pylewell Park defeated North Baddesley to become winners of the New Forest League Stone Cup evening knock-out competition for the third successive year. The picture shows John Williamson about to run out North Baddesley batsman, John Fisher.

Northwood C.C. 1st team, 1989, winners of the Bill Palmer Memorial League, 1989. Left to right (back): Roy Beale (umpire), Will Robins, Graham Long, Alan Gurney, Mark West, Mike Drury, John Brooks (umpire); (front) John Buckett (scorer), Keith Parker, Robin Evans, Andy Bull (captain), Darren Witcomb, Simon Goldsmith, Peter Came. 1st team players not present: Dave Reynolds, David Chetwood, Steve Lewis, Ron Denness, Robert Grove, Dave Mundell, Tony Lisher.

Bishop's Waltham Veterans v. Bishop's Waltham Ladies, 1989. The Club veterans declared at 197 for 9 (Fred Wiltshire 43, Tom Wilkie 27) and dismissed the Ladies XI for 87 (Alison Farrell 26).

Hampshire Under-19s, 1989. Left to right (back): Mat Smith, Martin Tidby, Mark Russell, Robert Hamber, Michael Trodd, Mat King, Barry Reed (team manager); (front) Ian Maynard, Darren Flint, Martin Kellaway, Jeremy Hayward, Ben Atwell, Jason Laney.

xxiv

Hampshire Club and Ground. A young K.S. Duleepsinhji made 70 of Trojans' 356 for 6 declared (A.F. Lewis 163 not out) against Basingstoke. Club sides were strengthened by players of County experience, among those to feature being M.B. Lawson, Frederick Weaver, General R.M. Poore and Herbert Blagrave. Touring clubs brought with them cricketers of character and distinction. At various times R.C. Robertson-Glasgow (with Oxford Authentics), A.J.L. Hill, Ronald Aird (recalling some fifty years later a 1926 innings of 187 runs for I. Zingari), E.H. 'Bunny' Tattersall (who kept wicket wearing an artificial leg), H.A. Dickens (Descendent of the Portsmouth-born novelist Charles Dickens, himself a known devotee of cricket), J.F. Anderson (183 in the 1928 Marlborough v. Rugby match at Lord's) and C. Bray appeared on Hampshire grounds.

Cricket weeks, particularly those on country estates, encouraged fixtures of a kind that would not be seen again outside of the 1920s and 1930s. There was an air of pageantry and festival, to which a variety of cricket caps and blazers made their own contribution.

An indifferent summer of 1922 saw an unusual number of 'scratched' fixtures, but would remain memorable for Hampshire's remarkable County Championship win over Warwickshire at Edgbaston. Having dismissed Warwickshire for 223, Hampshire were all out for 15 runs in less than 9 overs. Following on, Hampshire made 521, leaving the home side needing 304 to win, of which they managed 158. There is a report of a Hampshire player having apologized to his skipper for the first innings collapse, to which the Hon. Lionel Tennyson replied 'We must make five hundred next innings'. The rest is history.

The 1922 season was also historic for Purbrook C.C. At the opening of a new ground, ninety-two-year-old Mr G. White went out to receive the first delivery, having first played for the club seventy years earlier. Team photographs of the 1920s added a touch of history in that groups would often now include the scorer, equipped with a scoring book little different in size from those of sixty years later. A number of clubs in the 1920s and later also listed a 'telegraphist' or scoreboard operator, among their officials. As with ladies who provided and served match-day teas, recognition was being afforded to those whose work was often taken for granted.

Cricket in 1923 endured 'broken and varying weather' but in Hampshire at least produced some variety of achievement. Twenty-year-old D.A. Sibbick made 183 in 105 minutes (11 sixes and 21 fours) for Northwood II v. Ventnor II. In the Gosport League, W. Crockford for the Royal Clarence Yard at Salisbury, clean bowled the last 5 home batsmen in 5 balls to give his team a 4-run victory. The Stanford family (E.J. with 100 runs; C.H. taking 8 wickets for 44) played a major part in Breamore's win at St Giles. Hampshire Farmers, with 346 for 5 declared, defeated Berkshire Farmers by 151 runs. Alma were all out for 6 (Cook 8 for 2) against Langley Manor, one fewer than Rushington Park against the same opposition (J. Cook 7 for 1). Alton's B. W. Bentinck was in 1923 bowled by a ball deflected off a passing sparrow. Kent's opener Jack Bryan in making 236 against Hampshire at Canterbury hit a drive round the sight screen, on to a pavilion table, and into a picture of the Canterbury Week 1877, necessitating a new ball to replace the one that had become embedded with glass.

Very much part of the Hampshire cricket scene during the 1920s was the village game. Village cricketers had above all to be adaptable. Lloyd Budd, former Hampshire all-rounder and Test Match umpire, born at Hawkley, recalled having first become aware of cricket there from about the age of five. His later awareness tells us (in a letter to the author): 'In few cases were outfields mown much more than twice during the season, so the grass was often long with cow pats and horse manure much in evidence.' Away travel was often by way of bicycle, with Lloyd telling that: 'Bats and pads were strapped to the cross bar of the machine, batting gloves were not always worn and "boxes" unheard of.'

Also with a clear recollection of the village scene was Claude Crouch, club cricketer of wide experience and later umpire of high reputation. Of wicket preparation at Beaulieu, Claude wrote (in a letter to the author):

... in those early days before the start of the season a man with a horse was hired for the day to roll the square. The horse used to wear big leather boots, flat wooden bottoms with leather uppers strapped to the horse's leg to prevent its iron shoe damaging the turf.

Claude Crouch recalled East Boldre having played on a matting wicket laid on forest land in front of the parish hall. Before each match the matting had to be put in a place on a gravel base, the Forestry Commission not wishing anything firmer as it would then be considered to be of a permanent nature.

Foremost among Hampshire's cricket lore must be the 1924 appearance of Frederick J. Hyland for Hampshire at Northampton in a match restricted by rain to just 2 overs and 1 Northamptonshire run. Records show that F.J. Hyland neither batted nor bowled for Hampshire. An essay of delightful touch in Ronald Mason's *Sing All a Green Willow* conjectures that Frederick Hyland may have begun and ended his first-class career (he played for Hampshire only once having been a regular wicket-taker for Ringwood over the years) without having touched the ball.

In the 1925 season of generally mixed weather, in 268 first-class matches there were 60 totals over 400 and 78 under the 100 mark. Fordingbridge dismissed neighbours Martin for one run, and that, it was said, came from a missed catch. It was at this time understood that there were, in minor cricket, over sixty known instances of a team being out without a single run scored. At Southampton Parks in June 1926, York Building Boys' team bowled out Highfield School for 1 run, A. Bennett taking 6 wickets in 7 balls, helping to earn for his side medals provided by Mr J. Compton.

While leagues grew around 1926 and inter-village rivalry remained keen (C. Storer at 'well over fifty' took 6 for 1 in Godshill's dismissal of Woodgreen for 6 runs), Hampshire's stronger club sides were looking further afield. Deanery during 1926 made a week's tour of the Midlands, based at Dudley, a venture successful enough to encourage a tour to Eastbourne the following year.

Generally low scores during 1927 seem more likely to be a reflection of wet weather rather than an official reduction in the size of match balls to between 8 3/16 in. and 9 in. in circumference, the slightly reduced size having in any case been in use for some while. Phil Mead during 1927 registered his 100th first-class century. Isle of Wight all-rounder W.E.N. Scott played for the County in 1927 and was prior to his death in 1989 one of Hampshire's oldest living former first-class cricketers. Playing in 1927 for Walhampton in a 12-a-side match at Basildon, near Reading, Fred Kemish took 11 wickets for 3 runs, a feat he was able to look back on 20 years later when over 70 and still bowling out opposing batsmen.

Of impressive 1927 batting achievement, J.F. Keith and G.N. Daly, each with centuries, made an unbroken 218 for Claysmore School to 161 (C.S. Keith 6 wickets) from Deanery. At Minstead, in a game for boys of ten and under, Master Bob Darling's team (10 and 59) defeated Master Mark Pulteney's side (11 and 29). Less formally, a *Hampshire Advertiser* photograph of August 1927 shows a Southampton Common scene in which a small boy of perhaps seven or eight hits to mid-wicket while a similarly short-trousered lad stands, without gloves or pads, behind a set of five stumps without bails. In addition to press coverage, English cricket from 1927 would have the benefit of radio commentary, a field in which Hampshire-born John Arlott would make a lasting contribution.

Continuing to impress the Bournemouth scene in 1927 was Frederick Weaver, who for Lloyds Bank in the Bournemouth League took his overall 5000th wicket. Having during his Gloucestershire county days played with W.G. Grace, in thirty-eight years of cricket F.C. Weaver had also totalled over 29 000 runs.

After a noteworthy New Forest 'primrose' spring, 1928 produced a summer in which weather reports varied between accounts of violent storms and near record heat. During a season of record-making, for Hampshire Hogs against Free Foresters, Corinthian footballer C.B.G. Hunter made 283 (before falling l.b.w. to underarm bowler J.I. Piggott), passing the previous club best, 248 from A.H. Lewis v. the Green Jackets two years earlier. G.N. Daly reached 208 not out for Deanery v. Bournemouth.

Of bowling success during 1928, B. Wooldridge followed an unbeaten 101 for A.G.W.I. against R.A.F. Calshot with 6 wickets for 24, earning him the press accolade of 'man of the match', as might Bert Reade's 7 for 3 (including two hat-tricks) for Chandler's Ford in opposition to Braishfield. G. Dumper for Broughton took 8 for 14 against Nether Wallop, including an immediate hat-trick. For Bournemouth Amateurs in 1928, E.W. Marshall-Harvey in taking 203 wickets at 10.05 each in 586.3 overs, exceeded even his own high previous best.

The *Hampshire Advertiser* in January 1929 quoted from a letter by Arthur E. Knight, former Hampshire cricketer and Portsmouth footballer, concerning Walter Hammond. Earlier in Hammond's career, having seen him make a schoolboy 368 not out, Mr Knight wrote to recommend the young Hammond to Hampshire. While the County was, it seems, making up its mind, Gloucestershire stepped in and into their side, in due course, went one of the finest all-rounders to have played for England.

Hampshire cricket began 1929 in nostalgic manner with a Broad-halfpenny Down encounter between the Invalids, captained by J.C. Squire, and the Hampshire Eskimos skippered by E. Whalley-Tooker, playing in his final first-class match. The fixture was born, it was said, of a mild resentment that football should have invaded the cricket months of May and August. On a gloriously fine New Year's day the Invalids made 89 to win by 11 runs. The Hambledon Band played musical selections during the day, including 'The Cricketers of Hambledon', composed for the occasion by Peter Warlock, words by Bruce Blunt.

Among the fine-weather century-makers of 1929 were schoolmaster Jim Newman for Boldre, who imparted a love of cricket to generations of boys from the village, and a young Ted Drake from Southampton Parks, later to be taken on to the County staff and at football to make an outstanding mark as a Southampton, Arsenal and England centre-forward. There were bowlers' days also, Blokrete out 10 in Southampton Public Grounds League, St George's in the same competition making 9. For Bursledon Brickworks against Warsash Brotherhood II, D. Budden took 9 for 5. Taking the honours in South Baddesley's New Forest Elementary Schools' Cricket League winning team of 1929 (the sixth such success in 8 seasons), A. Metcalfe made 407 runs at an average 31.3, took 65 wickets at 4.35 and held 25 catches.

Southampton's A.J. Shield 1929 Parks Final drew a crowd of some 12 000 to watch Swallows make 110 (Sam Pothecary 45, F. Gross 5 for 57, P. Blackwell 5 for 19), Deanery 119 for 1 (T.V. Hollingworth 56 not out, J. Shearer 41) for a 9 wickets win. Basingstoke (now with Bert Butler and three sons in its ranks) tied with Crondall at 206 per side. There was a midsummer 1929 report that 'cricket for women is going ahead in Hampshire'. At a time when Ringwood was launching an appeal to purchase Carvers Field as a sports ground, ninety-three-year-old Mrs Hoskins recalled the town some seventy years earlier, saying 'we did not seem to have much time for amusements, but even then in Ringwood was a good bit of cricketing.'

The 1930s might be regarded in a number of ways as the golden age of Hampshire club cricket. The game flourished at all levels throughout the county, and benefited much from a fullness of press coverage. Match scores were allocated more than a full page in several of the county's newspapers, with local publications reporting similarly. Parish magazines also gave encouragement. 'Best of the Week' columns highlighted individual performances which were also noted in end-of-season summaries and published averages. Keeping careful record of the county side's fortunes in a scorebook of her own, Miss E. Cuthbert of Southampton followed Hampshire regularly not only at Southampton but at Portsmouth and Bournemouth also.

Development was in the 1930 air. General Poore captained Gentlemen of Hampshire against those of Dorset to mark the opening of an attractive new sports ground at Kinson, Bournemouth. St Catherine's Hill at Winchester, scene of Hampshire's first known cricket in 1647, was purchased by the Wykehamist Lodge of Freemasons for presentation to Winchester College. Aware of the need to provide an adequate view of the ball against a hedge and tree background, Fordingbridge Cricket Club spent £13 on a 'pair of sighting screens'.

Hampshire County Cricket Club, costing around £10 000 a year to run in 1930, granted a benefit match to Phil Mead, who recalled that the day he signed for Hampshire he received an invitation to join Surrey: a little too late! Also in Hampshire's colours during 1930, the prolific wicket-taker from Bournemouth, spin bowler Charles Fynn in his first ever county over captured the Lancashire wickets of Iddon and Taylor. At Southampton, Don Bradman, with the Australian tourists, just beat the rain to complete 1000 runs in May.

Among teams to provide 1930 reports, Southampton Rotarians, A.H. Curtis prominent with bat and ball, met opponents such as Portsmouth Rotary and Southampton Corporation (for whom Councillor E. Tolfree made an unbeaten hundred), while Southampton Clergy (Revd A.L. Bryan 86 of their 136 runs) drew with the Southampton Borough Corporation. Such fixtures would have been strong in friendship, a feature prominent in the increasing popularity of cricket club dinners during the 1930s. Dinners provided an opportunity for reminiscence, as with Bartley's first such annual occasion during 1930, when members recalled locally born Victor Norbury, who had gone on to play for Hampshire, Lancashire and Northumberland.

A number of notable Hampshire-connected names featured in the obituary columns of 1930. Widely mourned was Hampshire's much respected head groundsman, Jesse Hopkins, whose work at Southampton County Ground included the laying of 2000 new turves each year. William Penney, born near Hambledon ninety-one years earlier, had in his life scarcely ever missed a local village match in that vicinity. Nearing one hundred when he died, Canon Charles Theobald had played for Winchester v. Eton at Lord's during 1848; saved his brother from drowning in the Itchen; and ridden a horse at the age of ninety. James Gibb, a pioneer of ping pong, was seventy-six when he died in spring 1930 at Ventnor, Isle of Wight. Benning Arnold of Bournemouth lived until he was 106, having played bowls, it was said, at the age of 103. Mrs Anne Grace Russell, born at Portchester in 1823 and believed to be Hampshire's oldest woman, in November 1930 passed her 107th birthday.

The season of 1931 featured erratic, mainly damp, weather. Looking back some 150 years, Hambledon in August 1931 at Broad-halfpenny Down met H.M.S. *Nelson* in a match played wearing period costume, using two stumps, bowling lobs, and scoring by notches on a stick that was at the end sold for charity. Harry Weeks was in 1931 presented with an inscribed armchair in recognition of forty-one years as honorary treasurer to Southampton Public Grounds Cricket Association. Also casting his mind back to forty years earlier was Alfred Coward of Southampton, who had for Bassett against Eastleigh clean bowled ten opposing batsmen for 6 runs. Councillor A.E. Nield, seventy years old in 1931, that season bowled for 17 overs to take 7 for 30 in Brighton Corporation's victory over Portsmouth for a valuable gold trophy presented by Sir William Dupree, three times Mayor of Portsmouth.

Looking to the future, a September 1931 service for sportsmen at Over Wallop was conducted by the Revd G. Maurice Elliott, an advocate of Sunday games after completion of morning service. It would be a decade and more before the idea of Sunday club cricket gained any measure of acceptance, and then in the first instance brought about much by the altered circumstances of wartime.

1931 was memorable for Hampshire's opening batsman and outstanding fielder John Arnold, in that he opened England's innings against New Zealand, partnering Alfred Bakewell of Northants. At football, a winger of marked pace and scoring ability with Southampton and Fulham, John Arnold won an England soccer cap against Scotland in 1932-3, becoming one of a select band (not more than a dozen or so) to have been chosen for England at both sports.

Runs flowed during a 1932 summer of genuine heat, although against the general trend Ringwood Electricity Supply Company were dismissed for 1 run (a bye) by Mooney and Johnson of their West Hampshire counterparts. Among wicket-takers, Miss E. Myson and Miss D. Williams are each credited with reaching the hundred mark for Sherfield-on-Loddon.

Encouraged possibly by the warm dry season of 1933, Southampton Parks Final attracted a July evening crowd of some 10 000 to see All Saints out for 91 (C. Knott 7 for 28) and Deanery to a winning 96 for 4. The Southampton County Ground Knock-out Competition Final was watched by about two thousand people, Crows Nest out for 57 (A. Curtis 6 for 22), O.S.O. comfortably home with 71 for 1.

At Bournemouth and District Cricket League A.G.M. early in 1934, Melvill Druitt was elected President for the twenty-first year in succession, and retiring League Secretary Mr W.A. Sutton was pleased to refute an often heard remark that league cricket 'conduced to excessive keenness and bad sportsmanship'. During a mainly hard-wicket summer, former Harrow schoolmaster Mr C.G. Pope, by 1934 into his sixties, made 110 not out of New Milton's 223 for 7 declared to 155 from Trojans (B.R. Gleave 54). Dick Jenvey made an unbeaten 202 for Lymington at home to Aldenham in a two-day fixture, as a number of Cricket Week matches were at that time. Freddie Hewitt made 89 not out of

Walthampton's 178 for 5 declared against Exbury, and then took 5 wickets for 6 runs.

Village clubs welcomed the opportunity to test themselves against town opposition in evening knock-out competitions, with Lieutenant Edward Cadogan (of the Army and Hampshire) 131 not out (7 sixes, 14 fours) in a memorable innings for Beaulieu in the New Forest area Alderman Stone Cup. Winchester College cricketers had for twenty years from 1934 the benefit of coaching from former Sussex and England all-rounder Ted Bowley. The college had also enjoyed the instruction of Yorkshire and England cricketer E. Rockley Wilson. At Newport, Isle of Wight, fairground in 1934, a thirteen-year-old boy bowled at a coconut shy with an action, it was said, modelled on Harold Larwood. Almost every ball dislodged a coconut and with others asking him to bowl for them, eighty-seven were won before the stall holder, facing a nearly spent stock of coconuts, barred the lad from further competition.

Using cricket skills in a middle-1930s peace-keeping role was Captain Oswald Cornwallis, President of Froxfield C.C. from 1954 to 1973, and during the 1930s commanding H.M.S. *Scarborough* in the West Indies. Receiving Admiralty orders to visit an island where rioting had been reported, the captain sent a 'ship to shore' message challenging the islanders to a cricket match against the Royal Navy, with the happy result that cricket took precedence over rioting.

Struggling against the rain interruptions of 1936, Hampshire with its youngest county side for some twenty years rose from bottom to mid-table in the County Championship. The question of Sunday club cricket was again given an airing here and there, but the time had not yet come for what would be a fairly widespread adoption.

In an altogether sunnier 1937, Hampshire's captain R.H. Moore made 316 in 380 minutes against Warwickshire at Bournemouth, overtaking the County's previous first-class highest, 304 by R.M. Poore in 1899 during a season in which he averaged more than a hundred with the bat for Hampshire.

At a time when there was talk of plans to partly restore the 'Bat and Ball' at Hambledon, Surrey's Hambledon cricketers visited Hambledon in Hampshire to tie a match at 166 runs each. F. Hall made 50 for the home side and E. Parker for the visitors, who with 9 wickets down for 160, had F. Edwards hit a six before being bowled next ball.

While in 1937 a club such as Froxfield was from an income of £25 able to make a profit of £14, at Basingstoke running costs per season were around the £300 mark. Basingstoke in 1937 staged a match between the touring Australian women's team and West of England opposition, the game particularly remembered for an unbeaten double century from Miss Pat Holmes for the Australians.

Subject once more to rain interference, captained by Cecil Paris, later to become a major administrator at national and international level, Hampshire during

1938 broke new ground by playing Northants on the Island, at Newport. Hampshire overcame rain for Stuart Boyes to play a key all-round role and for Neil McCorkell to hit a winning six in the closing available minutes.

The cricket season of 1939 was played in an often unreal atmosphere against a background of European tensions that led in September of that year to the outbreak of the Second World War. The summer was wet, with only occasional spells of real sunshine. Among prominent Hampshire club sides were old Tauntonians (Walter Lancashire a stylish run scorer, Wally Prevett successful with the ball), Bournemouth Sports Club, and Bramtoco (Vic Guy 1043 runs at average of 37.25). Still in existence were old-established clubs such as Old Wykehamists (founded 1874), the Green Jackets (dating from December 1884, the original Minute books carefully preserved), and Hampshire Hogs (formed in 1887 as the Northlands Rovers Cricket Club). War shortened the season for a number of places. Ringwood and Somerley had planned in September 1939 to play a centenary repeat fixture, but the match gave way to the war situation.

8

Seasons of War 1940-1945

WHILST THERE HAD BEEN strong feeling during the 1914-18 war that sport should not be played at such a time, in 1940 there was general acceptance of the view that organized matches, as well as providing relaxation for Service personnel and others engaged in the war effort, would have a morale-lifting value.

The County Championship was discontinued, although a few informal inter-county games of limited duration were played. Hampshire's A.G.M. in March 1940 confirmed that there would be no county side in the field for a while. Stuart Boyes would, however, supervise junior coaching classes, and the Southampton Ground was to be available for club fixtures. Mr W.L. Sprankling was the County's acting hon. secretary.

A number of clubs throughout the county were able to operate after a fashion during 1940, among them Chilworth, Deanery, Ventnor, Romsey, Trojans, St Helens, Weeke, Longparish and Sway. The 8-ball over was in general use. Wartime restrictions on petrol, fuel, food and clothing had an impact on cricket. At some grounds iron railings were taken away to be used in the making of munitions.

Of the few competitions to function, Swallows were 1940 champions of the Southampton Public Grounds League, whose League Secretary Mr L. Green's unbeaten 107 for Crows Nest took 9 sixes and 5 fours off the Alma bowling. In the Bournemouth and District War League, noted former Boscombe footballer Ron Eyre took 8 Municipal wickets for 23 runs for his team Electric. At Winchester, where there was a Choirs Cricket League, the Mayor encouraged young men to keep fit in readiness for active service.

The Australian flag flew over Southampton Sports Centre during 1940 when an Australian XI made 152 for 7 after having dismissed Southampton Touring Club for 110. At Southampton County Ground, which suffered the collapse of a wall in January 1940, at a match in aid of the Red Cross, Harry Egerton's XI made 155 for 3 (Arthur Holt and Stan Broomfield their third successive century opening partnership) in defeating John Kemp's side, all out for 81 with Charlie Knott taking 8 for 40. In fine all-round form, H.A. Pawson made 100 not out and took 5 for 45 for Winchester College against Eton.

As a reminder of different times, the will of Walter Parsons, a noted former Southampton Parks cricketer, who had played for Hampshire in 1882, bequeathed his cricket bats to Southampton Public Grounds Cricket Association.

Hampshire club fixtures in 1941 were increasingly against Services XIs, who were able to include players of first-class standard, from time to time. Second Lieutenant J.H.G. Deighton, later to play for Combined Services and Lancashire, was a prolific wicket-taker for Northumberland Fusiliers. R.A.S.C. (O.C.T.U.) included Captain A.L. Hilder, formerly of Kent. Stan Squires of Surrey would later feature in R.A.F. XIs stationed in Hampshire, as would Manchester United footballer Charlie Mitten, gifted left-handed all-rounder at cricket.

John Arnold, double cricket/football England international, brought his Hampshire cricketing skills to emergency use during a spring 1941 bombing 'blitz' on Southampton. A large building was on fire and it was necessary to break a third-floor window so that water hoses could be brought into operation. The Fire Service had no means of smashing glass that high until John Arnold, serving then in the A.F.S., picked up half a brick from the roadway and sent it first time through the upper window, enabling firemen to use hoses to prevent the flames from spreading. A member of Totton Historical Record Society some forty-five years or so later had clear memories of having been on night-time Fire Service duties with John Arnold.

Forces teams were active in the Portsmouth area during 1942 when H.M.S. *Hornet* defeated H.M.S. *Victory* in the United Services Knock-out Cup Final. As part of Gosport's 1942 Stay-at-Home Holiday programme, a competition for seventeen teams (including Gosport Amateurs, the A.R.P., Home Guard, A.A., Camper & Nicholsons, and the Royal Marines) was won by the County Police.

Many in Portsmouth in 1942 mourned the loss of Roman Catholic priest Father Frederick Freely, M.C., a sportsman of international reputation and widely known in Portsmouth for his work in depressed areas.

Bournemouth's 1943 cricket season was away to an early start. On 16 March, in weather warm enough to encourage deck-chair spectators, an Air Forces match saw an Australian XI defeat New Zealand by 76 runs, with Keith Miller and Keith Carmody taking part, the hours of play being 1.30 p.m. to 4 p.m.

Hampshire's first wartime fixture, something of a reunion occasion, took place at the Southampton County Ground in August 1943, when Hampshire dismissed an Empire XI for 138 (L. Watkins 38, O.W. Herman 5 for 35) and then made 232 for 7 (Squadron Leader P.A. Mackenzie D.F.C., D.S.O., making 68, Arthur Holt 56, Major C.G.A. Paris 52 not out, L.D. Chadda 5 for 61).

Southampton Touring Club, at its pre-season 1944 A.G.M., re-elected Chairman Reg Fry and Captain/Hon. Secretary Harry Egerton to office, for each the twentieth successive year in these posts. At a members' 'get together', Southampton players and supporters were entertained in vigorous fashion by former Hampshire captain, Major Lord Tennyson, who recited verse that was, he said, 'definitely not written by my grandfather'. The cricketer's grandfather, Alfred, 1st Baron Tennyson, Poet Laureate in succession to William Wordsworth, lived for some years at Farringford, Isle of Wight.

Hampshire club sides, in 1944 playing with 6 ball overs, had to re-arrange planned fixtures at times during the season as Services cricketers became increasingly engaged in activities that would lead to the Allied Forces 'D-Day' landings in Normandy.

Playing for Basingstoke against R.A.F. Farnborough during 1944, R.C. Smith took 10 wickets for 8 runs, hitting the stumps each time. Retiring from active cricket at this time was Mr W. Maughfling, General Secretary of Thornycroft Athletic for twenty-five years and a player all told for fifty seasons. Also with an impressive all-round record, Norman ('Norrie') Stride, in 1944 Chairman of Southampton Public Grounds C.A. and connected with Parks cricket since his schooldays, held a personal eleven Parks' medals, with St Mary's and All Saints.

Hampshire's 1945 cricket scene was brightened by appearances of the British Empire XI, a team much associated with the name of Essex all-rounder Ray Smith. Cricket followers in a German Prisoner of War camp were able, through a German propaganda newspaper, to read of the Empire XI in Hampshire. While the Empire players were generally too strong for club opposition, Southampton Police defeated their visitors by 134 (Dr C.B. Clarke 7 for 62) to 108 (Bill Dodd 6 for 30; the Empire XI openers H.P. Crabtree and Ernest Eytle an opening 48 runs).

Police cricket flourished both on the Isle of Wight and mainland, where the Major St A.B. Warde Knock-out Competition was held. Three Southampton Police team members (J.C. Andrews, Lloyd Budd and L.C. Watkins) won places in the National Police side that met Club Cricket Conference at Lord's. Southampton Police took part in a rain-affected Whit Monday 1945 match with a Hampshire XI: Police 90 (H.G. Gibbons 19, G. Charrett 3 for 23, C. Knott 4 for 34). Hampshire 105 for 5 (Neil McCorkell 34, John Arnold 25).

Hampshire's own fortunes varied in two one-day matches with Sussex. At Southampton, Sussex made 148 (John Langridge 39, D. R. Fell 61, 'Lofty' Herman 5 for 39) and Hampshire 168 for 6 (Neil McCorkell 68, Arthur Holt 34, Leo Harrison 44, James Langridge 4 for 38). In the return at Hove, Sussex reversed matters convincingly, winning by 8 wickets.

Club cricket provided noteworthy achievements county-wide during 1945. Southampton Touring Club continued at strength, with established players such as wicketkeeper/batsman Reg Haskell supplemented by youngsters Jimmy Gray and Ralph Prouton. Southampton footballers Don Roper and Albert Roles made all-round contributions. Albert Roles had achieved the rare feat of a century with the bat in earlier years as a schoolboy for Deanery in the Southampton Elementary Schools League, as well as in the same season taken 8 wickets for 5 runs against Western School. Also making his 1945 mark, C.S. Camps made a century for Calmore against Saunders Roe, while with the ball Terence Walsh

(Churcher's College, Petersfield) took 8 for 2 against Portsmouth Grammar School.

Timely for the future, acknowledgement of cricket's grass roots came from Learie Constantine in a summer 1945 talk to Southampton Rotary Club. The noted West Indian cricketer stated his belief that the greatness of English cricket sprang from 'the village greens of England'. Former England captain Douglas Jardine, who as a boy had played cricket for Burley and in later life appeared again on the Burley ground, is known to have had high regard for the place that English village cricket held in the fabric of the game. 1945 saw the end of the war and victory was celebrated in city, town and village. Life would not in many ways ever be the same again.

9

Resumption and Flourish

THE SEASON OF 1946, one of rebuilding, was tackled with an enthusiasm that minimized the discomforts of generally unfavourable weather. The County Championship was resumed, with Hampshire under Desmond Eagar's leadership taking tenth place. Village and club sides were in many cases resuming after a gap of several years and needed to overcome restrictions on the acquisition of essential gear. The purchase of equipment was controlled, the supply of new balls was limited, while there was a waiting list for the re-blading of bats.

Against a background of difficulties to be overcome, there were team and individual performances of special note. Hambledon travelled to meet the Regency Club of Brighton and in a match of 4-ball overs, all underarm, played for an 18-gallon barrel of punch and lost by 183 runs to 174. For Basingstoke in their 252 to 13 win against Reading, Ratcliffe took 8 wickets for 7 runs. E.A. Ingram of Ealing C.C., in a 12-a-side game away to Bournemouth Sports Club, took all 11 home wickets for 57 runs. Hampshire's county cricketers, with a wealth of footballing experience, changed games to defeat the Aquitania by 11-0, the County line-up including John Arnold (Captain), Arthur Holt, Dick Court, Harry Lanham (winner of England schoolboy international caps at football), Reg Macey, 'Lofty' Herman, Tom Dean, Neville Rogers, Sam Pothecary, and Charlie Knott. With counties in the post-war years widening the field to strengthen their ranks, among prominent footballers whose names were mentioned in connection with Hampshire were Reg Halton (Bury wing-half) and Tommy Lawton (Everton and England centre-forward).

Southampton footballer Ted Bates, later to become 'Saints' manager and then director, was offered a Hampshire cricket trial, but football commitments had to come first. Ted Bates' father, William Bates, made more than 400 first-class cricket appearances for Yorkshire, Glamorgan and Wales, as well as football with Leeds United and Bolton Wanderers. Cricketer Billy Bates, Yorkshire and England all-rounder, whose name is inscribed in a verse on the Ashes urn, was grandfather to Ted Bates, whose sporting ancestry was fully upheld by more than fifty years at Southampton Football Club in a variety of much respected capacities.

Cricket in Hampshire took further recovery steps forward during the fine weather of 1947, with clubs able to resume some form of 'cricket week'. Umpire Fred Root had the experience, during the late-season 1947 Bournemouth Week, of standing in successive championship matches when Hampshire first of all tied with Lancashire and then drew with Yorkshire, for whom opener Len Hutton made an unbeaten 270 in six hours. Visiting the Isle of Wight, Hampshire made 449 (Gerald Hill a century, 6 wickets for Alan Weeks), to 72 and 114 for 5 from East Cowes. Successful with the ball during 1947, W. Jupe for Alresford took 100 wickets at less than 4 runs each, while for A.G. Payne's XI v. Hordle, J. Berry's 10 for 9 included two hat-tricks.

The widely known cricket writer 'Country Vicar', the Revd R.L. Hodgson, during 1947 retired from the post of vicar at South Baddesley in South Hampshire having lived in the village for more than twenty-nine years.

Hampshire in 1948 found many parts of the county taking part in organized cricket competitions. Andover's Knock-out Cup had a record thirty-three entries. Hyde Ramblers announced that Sir Anthony Titchborne had offered a 21 inch silver cup to the Winchester Club Cricket Association, with Ramblers as the previous year's Knock-out Cup winners becoming the first holders. Playing for Odiham London Road Boys' School in the North East Hants 1948 Schools League, L. Hicks took 104 wickets at 2.99 each, this in addition to having taken, by early August, 70 wickets for Odiham 2nd XI. In May 1948 Southampton Sports Centre reached its tenth anniversary, and in the decade survived wartime bombing, having staged 2108 cricket matches, 5276 games of football and 899 hockey fixtures.

The 1948 season saw some outstanding individual performances. Guy Jewell achieved the double of 100 wickets and 1000 runs for Basingstoke, a feat he was to repeat the following year. Alresford solicitor Ian Shield playing for Free Foresters took 10 first-innings wickets for 91 runs in a two-day match with Green Jackets at Winchester. John Mayman's 122 for Bramshaw included 8 sixes. G. Dunning made 19 of Durley's first innings 23 against Swestar Sports. In helping to dismiss Oakley for 6 runs, Hook's C. Gregory took 7 wickets without cost.

The successes of Winchester's Women's C.C. in 1948 included a narrow win by 53 (J. Parker 33) to 30 (J. Parker 6 for 7) against Reading University. A decade or so earlier, Winchester schoolmistress Miss Betty Snowball, an England Women's Test wicketkeeper of outstanding ability, had captained Hampshire Women in their match with the 1937 touring Australian Women.

Hampshire's county club was very much involved with the overall scene during 1948. Pre-season 'How to do it' demonstrations were held at Southampton's County Ground. Desmond Eagar with Sam Staples ran classes for junior members. An *Echo* photo showed John Arnold coaching fourteen-year-old Gerald Miller of Nursling. The county team, in 1948 making most of its away journeys by coach, exercised snooker skills against Southampton footballers, and sporting knowledge in a 'Twenty Questions' quiz with a Southampton C.C.A. team represented by Messrs H.C. Stevens, J.K. Andrews, A. Woodley and E.W.A. Croxford.

The 1949 weather improved after an indifferent start. Bert Butler of Basingstoke C.C. completed fifty years as the club's highly regarded groundsman. Bert Butler's playing career extended back to 1897 while during the period from 1901 to 1950, according to the club's excellent history and statistical summary, in the course of 856 appearances for Basingstoke he had made more than 21 000 runs and taken over 1830 wickets. Bert Butler was from a family who gave exceptional service to Basingstoke cricket, his own contribution being marked in 1949 with honorary life membership of the club, its first such award.

Playing in 1949 for Aldershot Services at home to the M.C.C., Major W.M.E. White scored two separate hundreds (112 and 120 not out), with all but one of the runs coming on the second day.

Monday 19 September 1949 was memorable for the players and large crowd at Dean Park, Bournemouth for the visit of the Duke of Edinburgh's XI to play the Hampshire XI. The County declared at 254 for 8, of which Neville Rogers made 93. The Duke of Edinburgh's team won with a wicket in hand, thanks largely to 80 from Stan Squires (Surrey) and 52 from Denis Compton. The Duke of Edinburgh bowled 9 overs of off spin to take 1 wicket for 25, and in his side's innings made 12 before falling to Gerald Hill. The scorer was Len Sprankling, with the match umpired by Messrs Sam Pothecary and Frank Chester. After the game there was a dinner at the King's Arms Hotel, Christchurch, where crowds gave the Duke of Edinburgh 'a tumultuous reception'.

The 1950s proved to be a transitional period for many Hampshire cricket clubs. Players and officers remaining from the pre-war years were in some cases wishing now to step down, creating a need for replacements. On a 1950 Sunday fixture, Winchester Women declared at 121 for 3, then dismissed Romsey Women for 8. On the same day, at Weeke, Castaways made 25, putting Y.M.C.A. out for 7 (T. Sowerby 6 for nought, B. Mortimer 4 for 6) and 7 again (T. Sowerby 5 for 4, B. Mortimer 4 for 1), Castaways choosing not to change bowlers in an overwhelming win. Among the runs at Hordle, were Eddie Saunders with a century for Rydal against L.D. Chadda's XI for whom Indian Test player C.T. Sarwate made 76 not out.

Playing Hampshire club cricket during 1951 was Denys Roberts, later to become in 1989, as Sir Denys Roberts, President of the M.C.C. Others to enjoy the season were Ken Biddulph (later to take 270 wickets for Somerset) with R.A.F. Calshot, and Wally Scott (517 runs averaging 103.40 and 65 wickets at 5.73) in the Hartwells' side that won the Bournemouth Business Houses 1951 League title. At Bournemouth's Dean Park in July 1951, Amy Hudson and Joan Schmidt, each with centuries, opened with a stand of 200 for the Australian

Women, the West of England Women making 110 and 141. During the 1951 Hampshire v. Gloucestershire meeting at Portsmouth, a delivery from Charlie Knott to Sir Derrick Bailey 'struck and killed' a butterfly. Two seasons earlier on the occasion of Chichester's visit to Ampfield, a Romsey batsman hit a 6 out of the field, the ball landing on a goose with fatal consequences.

Welcoming a 1952 season of improved weather, Lymington all-rounder Arthur Smith marked his twenty-fifth year with the club with a series of outstanding performances. The compiler of these pages on Hampshire cricket, first as a boy and then as a man, learned much about cricket from such Lymington players as Arthur Smith, Joe Walsh, Mike DuPre, Dick Jenvey, and Jack Williams, together with Umpire Jim Ridgeway and long-serving Hon. Secretary Len Hoare. Opponents including Lloyd Budd, Arthur Holt, Fred Figgins, Jack Hull, George Cotton, Harold Pearce, Phil Pick, Dick Carty and George Green were among those always well worth listening to. Much of the lore of club cricket is passed on by word of mouth. Those were rich years for listening.

Coronation Year 1953 was marked by cricket celebration competitions, often in the face of generally unfavourable weather. The County Cricket Club, although low (fourteenth) in the championship table, in a summer of Australian visit enjoyed its best season financially. The membership was 4644; over 100 000 spectators paid at the gate and a profit of £1930 was made. Of individual pleasure in 1953, bowling for Lymington 2nds against Pylewell Park, left-arm pace bowler Ken Savill took all 10 wickets for 4 runs. Having during the 1944-5 football season scored 10 goals in a match for Lymington Rovers v. a Royal Artillery XI, Ken Savill achieved the certainly rare, and possibly unique, distinction of taking 10 wickets and scoring 10 goals for the clubs of one town.

Club fixtures of 1954 were subject to an unwelcome level of rain cancellation. Braving all were the youngsters of Forest Wagtails in their second season. Organized by Hugh Crofton, an outstanding example of cricket commitment, the senior lads played eighty matches during 1954, and the 2nd XI around half that number. Also in the New Forest area, New Milton's team to win the local Alderman Stone Cup competition included Ian Wooldridge, a spirited left-handed batsman, later to become a journalist of international reputation. In his book *Travelling Reserve*, Ian Wooldridge tells entertainingly of his experience as a young cricketing hopeful facing the bowling of Hampshire's leg spinner Tom Dean, whom he was to meet in later life under entirely different circumstances.

Obliged after the 1953 season to find a new home, Cadnam C.C. was granted, by the Forestry Commission, an area of New Forest wasteland covered with gorse to a height of 4 feet, a virtual swamp. Ron Biddlecombe, through the pages of Cadnam's cricket history from 1800 to 1980, tells something of the mammoth undertaking to clear the site of some 4 acres and to have it ready for match play by June 1956. Among those to be praised for an operation that was very much a team effort was George Jewett, a footballer and cricketer of ability, who when his playing days were done put a great deal back into both games. Cadnam Cricket Club was certainly in the tradition of self-help that has marked the game over the centuries. Travellers entering the Forest can now see a ground and pavilion of excellent appearance, a lasting tribute to those who worked so hard.

The fine weather and successful cricket (the team rose to third place) of 1955 brought the county club a welcome financial boost. Ironically, during a season of often ideal conditions, in May 1955 R.A.F. Calshot's game with Hythe and Dibden was stopped by snow and rain. Beyond interruption were the cricketers of the Rydal Club, near New Milton who, with promotion to Bournemouth League Division One in 1955, had risen from the Fourth Division in six seasons becoming, it was said, the first side to have played in all four divisions.

County cricket came to Cowes, Isle of Wight, in 1956, when Hampshire met and drew with Worcestershire at the J. Samuel Whites Ground. During the summer a cricket exhibition attracted 16 000 visitors to the Bargate Museum at Southampton, by courtesy of the Mayor and Corporation. Also treading new paths in 1956, the Cricket Society XI travelled to Hambledon to meet Ablative Absolutes on Broad-halfpenny Down, losing by 76 to 75.

The 1956 season was wet, producing some 'staggering low totals'. Nothing could detract though from Guy Jewell's 166 wickets for Basingstoke, including all 11 against Ian Bedford's XII. At Pennington, the vicar, the Revd John Biddell Southbourne hit a rapid 147, believed to be the highest score on the ground, within sight of Yaldhurst House, former home of the celebrated England and Corinthian footballer G.O. Smith. For Penninton v. Chandler's Ford, Michael Pardey's unbeaten century included four successive sixes.

Cricket's programme for 1957 was once again rain interrupted, albeit there were days of real heat. *The Official History of the Hampshire County Cricket Club* was published in 1957. Of the joint authors, Harry Altham brought his love of history to bear on the years to 1915; John Arlott wrote with knowledge and affection of the seasons from 1919 to 1939; Desmond Eagar from his experience as captain and secretary was able to write in depth of the period from 1945 to 1956 inclusive. Roy Webber provided the statistics so valuable to such a work.

Among the grounds written about in the *History* was Dean Park, Bournemouth, a place rich in tradition. Mrs E.A. Miller has recalled the sense of occasion during the pre-war 'July Week' when on 'Ladies Day' the wives of captain and amateurs would arrive in their 'Ascot' gowns. Dean Park has a pavilion enclosure where players and members can meet and mingle. During the lunch interval on the first day of Hampshire's 1957 match with Northants, Frank Tyson sat on an outside window ledge, cap pushed back from forehead, reading a paperback book. When a cricket enthusiast approached him for conversation, Frank Tyson put his book to one side and listened. Behind him in the Hampshire dressing room sat Philip Mead, then blind, eating a sandwich and tomato. Hampshire cricketer Alan Rayment asked the former Test player 'Are you all right there, Phil?' Another former great all-rounder, Wilfred Rhodes, retired to the Bournemouth area and was often at Dean Park matches of this time. The legendary Yorkshireman was usually to be seen in the front row of the pavilion's balcony seating.

Cricket has been subject to all manner of interruptions. At Lord's in June 1957 play was stopped by a plague of insects that troubled Hampshire batsmen Jimmy Gray and Henry Horton before moving on to annoy the 17 000 crowd at the Oval. During Kent's August 1957 match with Hampshire at Canterbury, play was held up when a mouse chased after a four by Vic Cannings and narrowly missed being trodden on by Colin Cowdrey. The schoolboy owner of the mouse eventually resolved the situation by diving and catching the creature in his cap.

E.W. Swanton has described the English summer of 1958 as 'among the most liquid and gloomy within memory'. The season was brightened for Hampshire by the County coming second in the championship, and for the choice of Roy Marshall with Derek Shackleton among Wisden's 'Five Cricketers of the Year'.

Ian Burt's history of Froxfield Cricket Club tells of a 1958 occasion when during an away fixture with Twyford, four of the home fielders dashed from the field at the sound of a distant fire-alarm siren. Twyford's captain recruited four spectators to make up the fielding number and continued with the game. Also in 1958, having been dismissed for 43, Froxfield put Soberton out for 6 runs and sought to play a second innings, to find that only the last two Soberton batsmen and their captain remained on the ground. During 1958, when Froxfield played thirty-one matches, skipper Reg Barnett took 134 wickets at 5.92. Reg Barnett among some 2000 wickets for Froxfield in all, achieved further hundred hauls in 1976 and 1977, in each of those seasons he attained a personal 'all ten'. Among many items of interest in the Froxfield history, Miles Tomalin relates an account of fixtures with Brief Candles C.C., a name inspired by Shakespeare's dramatic 'Out, out, brief candle'.

George Crouch, powerful Sway Batsman, would long remember the 1958 Alderman Stone Cup competition. Dropped first ball versus the New Forest Police, Crouch went on to an unbeaten 84 out of Sway's winning 93 for 2, then against further opponents Esso (Fawley) made 80 not out of his side's victorious 108 for 9.

The death occurred in 1958 of Canon John Glennie Greig, former Army and Hampshire cricketer of distinction, Secretary of the County Cricket Club 1921-30, and President 1945-6. In 1935 J.G. Greig was ordained in Rome as a Catholic priest and became Ringwood's first Father, having the Priest's House built, it is said, from his Army gratuity. Phil Mead, one of Hampshire's finest cricketers, died at Boscombe in March 1958. In one of her verses contributed to the Club Handbook, Imogen Grosberg sums up admirably in a few lines something of Philip Mead at the batting crease and with thought for the future: 'Unfussed, yet kingly, marching to his goal, But for the winter, one more "ton" of coal'.

The season of 1959 brought to a close, in splendidly sunny fashion, a decade that had featured miserably wet cricketing summers. The County Cricket Club enjoyed a number of 1959 landmarks. Harry Altham, Hampshire's President since 1947, was in 1959 nominated M.C.C. President. An indoor cricket school opened at the Southampton County Ground, and the 2nd XI entered the National Championship competition. Leo Harrison made 83 wicketkeeping dismissals, creating a Hampshire record. In the county at large, there was a growth in the level of colts cricket, leading in time to the strengthening of club ranks.

10

The Sixties and Seventies

MANY HAMPSHIRE CLUBS IN the early 1960s addressed themselves to the task of promoting colts cricket. Club scores in 1960, a rain-damaged season, showed names who through the years had made a full contribution to the sport. Crawley made 78 (T. Fullick 5 for 32), Easton and Martyr Worthy 80 for 4 (D. Fullick 38). Southampton Wednesday declared at 212 for 7 (Badminton 103 not out) and dismissed Hyde Ramblers for 160 (Stratton 60 not out, Risbridge 58). R. Clark made 77 of Deanery's 129 and with Noel Fisher taking 4 for 12, West End were bowled out for 89. Ray Budd (Old Tauntonians), Frank Burton (Brockenhurst) and Alf Strong (Milford) were also among the runs. For Rydal against Wellworthy, Reg Everett made 30 of his side's 61 for 9, then took 6 wickets (including a hat-trick) without cost in Wellworthy's dismissal for 44.

Hampshire in 1961 became County Champions for the first time, winning 19, drawing 6 and losing 7 of 32 matches to finish 18 points ahead of runners-up Yorkshire. In his book *Many a Slip*, Captain Colin Ingleby-MacKenzie regarded the success as a 'triumph for team spirit, a much hackneyed phrase in the often selfish business of professional sport'. *Wisden* in its summary of the achievement concluded that 'Holt's Colts' certainly played a vital part. Among the congratulations received by Hampshire were those of former England cricket captain Percy Chapman, who was to die at Alton a few days later in September 1961. As a boy, A.P.F. Chapman had attended Fritham House School in Hampshire, where his father, Mr F.E. Chapman, a considerable cricketer himself, was headmaster. *Hampshire C.C.C.'s Handbook* for 1961, good value at 2 s., contained a number of informative articles, including 'Hampshire and the M.C.C. Collection' by M.C.C. Curator, Diana Rait Kerr.

After the glories of its championship year Hampshire, in 1962, dropped to around halfway in the table, injuries contributing to the decline. Encouraging for the future, the 2nd XI had players of promise. The Castle Cricket Club of Winchester in 1962 marked its fiftieth anniversary. Vice-captain, in its inaugural season of 1912, was H.M. (Bert) Sherry, later to become Hampshire's first County Librarian.

Hampshire County Cricket Club in 1963, against a background of disappointing weather, celebrated the centenary of its present formation. The county played a closely fought defeat against an M.C.C. All England XI. At the centenary dinner in September 1963, a letter was read from E.A. (Ted) English, born on New Year's Day 1864, later to celebrate his own hundredth birthday in excellent health and well able to recall his Hampshire playing days. Bert Earney wrote in the Southampton *Echo* of Andover's 1963 centenary, recalling feats such as that of Tom Richardson (Surrey and England) taking all 10 Basingstoke wickets, the last 7 in successive deliveries, and batsman Bruce Lamb's innings of 250 not out in less than two and a half hours.

Enlivening the 1964 Hampshire club scene were former and present league footballers Harry Penk, Ken Wimshurst, Terry Simpson, Brian Clifton and Sam Stevens in the Husband's (Marchwood) team. Godfrey Evans, former Kent and England wicketkeeper, was appearing for New Milton. Colts cricket continued to develop. Youngsters in Lyndhurst 2nd XI had encouragement of former Hampshire all-rounder Gerald Hill, singled out for praise in the autobiography *How's That* of Test umpire Frank Chester. After a 1964 Lyndhurst match in which his skills were plainly still there, Gerald Hill said, 'You still enjoy it when the sun shines.'

Adding to cricket's memorable moments, batting for Winchester in the 1965 match with Harrow, R.L. Burchnall was struck on the head by a bouncer from C.A. Holt. The batsman's cap fell on to the stumps where, the umpire told, 'it hung suspended as though from a peg in the dressing room, without dislodging a bail.' R.L. Burchnall continued his innings to make 141.

By 1966, Hampshire club sides might expect to pay ground rent of £100 or more. Among the other expenditure would feature polyarmoured bats, to become increasingly popular. At a time when top-class pace bowlers were being measured as delivering at around 80 m.p.h., club batsmen too had difficulties. For Ellingham against Agrarians, Mike Montgomery took 10 wickets for 1 run, then made the 5 runs needed for Ellingham's win. Ray Flood, formerly of Hampshire and latterly of splendid service to Lyndhurst, in his 83 for Lyndhurst v. Lymington hit a high ratio of 8 sixes. For Minstead in 1966, Roy Hurst achieved the double of 1000 runs and 100 wickets.

County cricket was during 1967 played on Sundays, with Essex against Hampshire at Ilford in May 1967 reported as the first county match to begin on a Sunday. Among the season's exceptional club feats Bob Keeping, for Mudeford II against King's Park II, took all 10 wickets for 16 runs.

1968 brought a number of distinctions to Hampshire cricket. Cecil Paris was elected first Chairman of the Test and County Cricket Board, and another former Hampshire player, Ronald Aird, was nominated President of the M.C.C. Barry Richards in his Hampshire debut season scored 2314 runs and in the county's 68-run win against a Rest of the World XI took 7 second-innings wickets for 63 runs. The year also saw the formation of the Hampshire Exiles Club. Late in August 1968, Gosport schoolboy Paul Brown achieved mention in the national press. *The*

Times reported that spectators at Hampshire's Portsmouth match with Nottinghamshire heard a warning issued to Paul not to eat his lunchtime sandwiches, 'the sausages are off'. Paul had already eaten three of the sandwiches with no ill-effect, but was invited to complete his lunch as guest of the County Cricket Club in the Members' room.

The season of 1969 saw further 'firsts'. Hampshire finished second in the newly formed John Player League, Sunday afternoon limited-overs cricket. The Trojans were the first winners of the *Southern Echo* Cricket League. Single-wicket competitions became increasingly popular, and colts leagues flourished.

Hampshire cricket began the 1970s with thoughts of league competition increasingly in the mind. The 1970 Southern League in its second season saw Old Tauntonians, under the captaincy of Tony Baker and much indebted to the all-round performances of Derek Tulk, take the title from Trojans. Old Tauntonians during 1970 also claimed the Southampton Parks K.O. Hector Young Trophy, the Hampshire County Ground Knock-out Cup, and the Hampshire Challenge Cup.

Desmond Eagar in 1971 wrote with feeling about 'changing times', true of cricket at many levels in the decade under way. Here and there concern was being expressed at standards of club umpiring, reflecting perhaps the attitude of players to increased competitiveness as well as valid criticism of umpires. The debate did however re-emphasize the importance to cricket of umpires, working, as they now increasingly would, with scorers, for whom league requirements made their own task more demanding.

The county club, under the leadership of Coach Geoff Keith, with major contributions from Peter Ryan, Richard Lewis, David Turner and Danny O'Sullivan, won the 2nd XI Championship for the first time. The 2nds also played a drawn match against an England Women's XI, captained by free-scoring Rachel Heyhoe. At club level, the value of bar facilities as a contribution to after-match relaxation, as well as to finances, was becoming increasingly recognized.

Advertising and sponsorship would become a growing feature of the 1970s, with adverts thoughtfully used in the *New Forest Club Cricket Association's Handbook* for 1971, an organization continuing the foundations so firmly laid by Vic Loveless and Vic Trippick among others. In addition to statistical and other information, the *Forest Handbook* contained articles of historic value. F.E. Chapman's 'Bramshaw Days' was reprinted from an earlier *Cricketer Spring Annual*. An essay on Swan Green tells not only of the mighty oak a few paces away from the wicket there, but also of club stalwarts such as 'Chick' Warwick, in his time captain, coach, caterer, groundsman, player and much else. Dick Galton's excellent and well-illustrated brief history of Lyndhurst cricket makes a fitting conclusion to the resumption of a handbook that had been obliged to miss a year after issue 5.

Reminiscences play a valuable part in cricket history, as with John Grigsby's

'Boundaries of Memory' in the *Hampshire* magazine of June 1972. The recollections of former players are possibly not fully recognized as a source of historical worth. Sometimes the opportunity is not fully taken, as with this compiler's own earlier conversations with former Lancashire all-rounder Len Parkinson.

For many Hampshire club sides, 1972 would be the last season of its kind in that from the 1973 start of the Hampshire Cricket League there would be increasing emphasis on that form of play, new to the experience of many of those taking part. Already well established in the league scene, Rydal playing Christchurch in Bournemouth Division One suffered a remarkable collapse. Having dismissed Christchurch for 62 (Gary Robertson 7 for 21), Rydal went to 26 without loss prior to tea. They then lost 10 wickets for the addition of but one further run, David Paramore making 20 of the 27 total. As a reminder of the occasion, Rydal scorer Sid Charman framed and placed an immaculate score sheet in Rydal's new pavilion of years to come.

Hampshire in 1973 became County Champions for the second time, winning 10 and drawing the remaining 10 of their 20 championship matches. Only thirteen players appeared in championship fixtures: Richard Gilliat (captain), Gordon Greenidge, Barry Richards, Peter Sainsbury, David Turner, Mike Taylor, Andy Murtagh, Bob Stephenson, Danny O'Sullivan, Trevor Jesty, Bob Herman, Richard Lewis and Tom Mottram.

Encouraged by fine weather, 1973 also saw the beginning of the Hampshire Cricket League, the inaugural season marked by the first of a series of excellent handbooks. The 1974 handbook account of Kingsclere Cricket Club, dating from 1774, mentions that Percy Ford and John Ford, father and grandfather respectively of Geoffrey Ford, Hampshire C.C.C.'s Chairman, were prominent figures at Kingsclere earlier in the century. New Milton, captained by former Hampshire pace bowler David 'Butch' White, became the 1973 Hampshire Cricket League's County Division first champions, unbeaten in 13 fixtures, 2 of which were 'no decision matches'. Other title honours went to Lymington (County Division Two), with Alton Town (North Regional), Kingsclere (Mid Hants), Crofton (South Hants), with Old Portmuthians (who also won the League's 1972/73 quiz competition) heading the Supplementary Division.

Jack Hull in 1974 marked his fiftieth consecutive season as a Brockenhurst cricketer, in addition to which he had made a valuable contribution to Brockenhurst football, cricket, and village life in a variety of secretarial and other capacities. Hampshire cricket is noted for men and women who have given exceptional service over long periods of time. Without them the game's structure could not have been as it was. Of present-day achievement, in Bournemouth League Division Four, Laurie Ferrigi for Mudeford 2nds took 5 for 47 in the dismissal of Ensbury Park 2nds for 161, then of Mudeford 2nds' 121 made 100, the next highest score being 6.

Hampshire's county side in 1975 became John Player League winners for the first time. Simon Rowley, an all-rounder with Burley C.C., compiled an absorbing centenary year handbook, *Burley Cricket Club, 1875-1975*, for a club rich in history. Alive also to the future, Burley was prominent in colts cricket, with spin bowler John Stimson carrying out much valuable coaching work among the young of Burley and beyond.

League cricket in the county gathered pace during 1976, a summer of exceptional heat. In the Hampshire League, Hythe and Dibden succeeded AWRE as Division One champions, with Paultons, captained by Clive Dunning, taking the Second Division title. Divisional honours went to Park Lane, Compton & Shawford, Milford, Basingstoke & North Hants, and Welford Park. The league played a number of representative matches, including a high-scoring defeat (262 for 2 declared, to 248) against Middlesex League. Havant retained the Southern League Senior Championship, with the club also taking the 2nd XI title of the competition in its fourth year.

The Hampshire Cricket Association was reorganized in 1976. The Hampshire Cricket Society, to prove a forum for stimulating meetings, a source of excellent published newsletters and in general an organization for the encouragement of cricket interest, dates from 1976. Another valuable aid to maintaining all-year enthusiasm for the game was the introduction during 1976 of an indoor six-a-side competition based at Fleming Park, Eastleigh.

The season of 1977 has in some quarters been termed a 'summer of discontent'. During a year in which the weather did little to help, Hampshire club cricket continued to prove enjoyable. Deanery won the Southern League's Senior Division, with Trojans taking the *Echo* Trophy. The League's overall strength would be emphasized by success gained in representative competition.

Colin Savage succeeded Mr L.W. Long as Hampshire Cricket League Secretary for the 1977 season. The *League Handbook* for 1977 struck a number of encouraging notes, although President Richard Gilliat, the county-side captain, expressed concern that cricket was in danger of dying in many schools. It was increasingly important to encourage young players in all possible ways. The *League Handbook*'s 1977 cover showed left-hander Dennis Luff displaying the positive style that had brought him 832 North Division runs in 1976, at an average of 69.33. The pages contained a profile of Portsdown C.C., and a study of Hursley Park all-rounder Bill Fielder - 1114 games for the club over twenty-nine years; 16 465 runs, top score 109, with 68 half centuries and 92 'ducks'; 2889 wickets at 7.78 and 676 catches taken. As well as admiration for such a level of sustained performance, credit must be given to whoever was responsible for collating the statistics.

During the 1977 Winter, Indoor League competition grew, bringing a new element into the game of many cricketers. Colts cricket seemed to some extent to be making good the lack of opportunity in some schools. All of which added to renewed enthusiasm to greet the season of 1978, a year during which Hampshire, for the second time in Sunday competition, won the John Player League.

Gosport Borough in 1978 became the first Hampshire club side to reach the John Haig Trophy semi-finals, going out to eventual winners Cheltenham. Hampshire Cricket Association won the National Cricket Association County Knock-out Competition in the face of strong opposition, defeating Northamptonshire in a rain-affected, low-scoring final at Ealing.

Celebrations were well earned county-wide during 1979, helping to offset what has been labelled a 'soggy spring and dreadful summer'. The Southern League had successfully completed a sponsorship deal with the Town and Country Building Society. The Southern League's representative XI won the Truman Club Cricket Conference Inter-League Cup. Middlesex County League made 169 for 9 in their allotted 45 overs, the Town and Country Southern League reaching 170 for 1 in 39 overs ('Man of the Match' John Harris 95 not out and Alan Williams an unbeaten 46). Longparish became 1979 Hampshire League Division One champions, with other title honours spread among Follands, Easton & Martyr Worthy, United Services Portsmouth, Road-Sea, Sparsholt, Crown Taverners and Donnington.

Recognition of the important art of groundsmanship came with the Hampshire Cricket Society's award for 'Hampshire Club Ground of the Year', won in 1979 by Hampshire League club, Falkland C.C. of Newbury. Ernie Knights, Hampshire's head groundsman at the Southampton County Ground since 1947, and with the club years before that, died in July 1979. Hampshire Secretary A.K. 'Jimmy' James described Ernie Knights as a man 'completely devoted to the County Cricket Club'.

Appropriate to the New Forest's 900th Anniversary in 1979, cricket played a part. A New Forest XI met and was defeated by a celebrity side, which made 229 for 5 (John Chumbley 60) to the Forest's 189 (Ben Lyon 55, Jimmy Gray 5 for 40). Very much part of the Forest scene, Wally Shutler completed fifty years with Ellingham (formerly Somerley) Cricket Club. Les Parker reached a similar milestone with Woodgreen. Ending the year, in December 1979, New Forest C.C.A. Colts presentation evening was enriched by a talk from noted cartoonist 'Oz', who then drew cartoons with cricketing themes for the youngsters.

73

11

Into the Eighties

HAMPSHIRE CRICKET ENTERED THE 1980s with plenty of direction and purpose, despite the county side occupying bottom championship place in 1980. Throughout the county, league and cup competitions were becoming firmly established, building up their own character and colour. Sponsorship during the 1980s became increasingly part of the club scene. Winter indoor leagues on mainland and Island met a growing need at all levels. Grounds and premises were in many cases subject to overhaul and improvement, sometimes sponsor-aided, at other times individually supported. 'Friendly' fixtures during the 1980s would become very much associated with Sundays and mid-week. Touring sides remained attracted to Hampshire as a base for stays of up to a week. Hampshire clubs in turn ventured some distance on their travels, abroad on occasions.

New Year's Day 1980 saw the traditional fixture between Burley and a visiting Jack Frost XI, played this time on a matting wicket against a setting of a snow-covered outfield. The summer itself, although wet and cold in the main, was unforgettable for a number of Hampshire clubs. Gosport reached the Lord's final of the John Haig Trophy, with Jim Stares Gosport's 'Man of the Match'. Although losing to Marchwiel at Lord's in the Whitbread Village Championship Final, Longparish took some consolation from retaining the Hampshire League Division One title, a feat to be repeated in 1981. Longparish also received the 1980 Hampshire Cricket Society Award for the best kept club ground within county competition, with Longparish groundsman and umpire Ken Ball a well-deserving recipient of plaque and cheque from Society Patron John Arlott.

Off the field, Basingstoke & North Hants (captained by Derek Pyne) and Tilehurst C.C. (captain, Graham Edge) were joint winners of the 1980 Sports Quiz. John Arlott, through writing, radio and television so much a part of cricket in a great many homes throughout the world, retired from regular broadcasting in 1980. John Woodcock of Longparish (where his father the Revd Woodcock was in his time captain, chairman, treasurer and president of Longparish C.C.) was at the end of the 1980 season appointed editor of *Wisden*.

The 'Grass Roots' summaries in the *Hampshire County Cricket Club Handbook* of

74

1982 provided wide-ranging accounts of the county's club and colts scene during 1981. Contributors Desmond Hayward (Hampshire Cricket Association), Colin Savage (Hampshire Cricket League), Mike Vimpany (Town and Country Southern League), 'Pop' Marshall (Hampshire Schools C.A.) and Frank Bailey (Hampshire Cricket Society) were ideally fitted from their own experience to convey how much was happening in various directions. Among achievements to be highlighted were 10 wicket hauls each for Hampshire League bowlers Derek Eggbear (Thatcham) and Bob Jenkins (Purbrook), the first in the league's history. Mrs Janet Lees of B.A.T. at Totton, received the Hampshire Cricket Society's 1981 Ground of the Year award. John Barnard of Richard Taunton School at Southampton had early encouragement in 1982 with his selection for the English Schools' Cricket Association coaching course in April. A comparatively dry summer saw a number of Hampshire Cricket League trophies go to new homes. Among clubs successful in this direction were Emsworth (South East II), Sparsholt (South West I), Wellow & Plaitford (South West II), Linkenholt (North I), while Basingstoke & North Hants IV took the North II title, emulating a feat accomplished by the club's 3rd team in the 1976 season. Evidence of the league's progress was the extent to which a number of clubs advanced upwards to win titles in other divisions. Also making a welcome climb, the county team, captained for the second season by Nick Pocock, made a firm recovery to finish seventh in the championship.

Curdridge's score book for 1982 contained the entry 'balloon stopped play'. A huge grey-and-white hot air balloon had been used to advertise the opening of a new burger restaurant in Southampton. Lifting off from the city's Palmerston Park, pilot Tony Bolger of Calmore had intended coming down in the Wickham area. The day's heat made for rapid use of fuel and prompted a more rapid descent. The pilot chose Curdridge Cricket Ground in preference to a nearby wood, and made his landing on the playing strip. Royal Marine Commando Michael Hillier, on home leave, whose twin brother was in the field for Curdridge, took a photograph of the occasion. The list of reasons for interruption of play is rich and varied. Curdridge added a further historic line.

In winning the Town and Country Southern League Championship in 1983, Lymington set records that would be hard to beat, dropping only 8 points out of a possible 280 in 14 matches, all of which were won. Captained by Jon Hardy, the side included Stephen Andrew (later to play for Hampshire), and Andy Jones, in due course to become a successful Test batsman for New Zealand. The Hampshire Cricket League tables for 1983 showed club strength in North Hampshire and Portsmouth in particular. The Noel Fisher Memorial Trophy, bearing the name of the league's founder-chairman, went to Road-Sea, in the closest of finals against holders Longparish.

Mindful of links with the past, Hampshire Cricket Society members in October 1983 made a 'pilgrimage' to Broad-halfpenny Down and the Bat and Ball Inn at

Hambledon. They paused en route to visit the grave of Thomas Lord at West Meon, who after a cricket career including association with the ground that bears his name, retired to farm in Hampshire, where he died in 1832.

The hot dry summer of 1984 saw Hampshire League honours go once more in some part towards the Portsmouth direction, but here and there, healthy for the competition, new names were taking their place in the honours lists.

Vic Loveless in his Chairman's Report for the New Forest Club Cricket Association's 1984 handbook expressed concern at out-of-season 1983-4 'happenings'. Vic Loveless wrote of:

...the calamitous decision by the Verderers to insist that four of our swamp infested grounds be opened to forest animals for three months from October to December and a charge of £10 for the other three months be made when they were closed - a parody of closing the gate after the horse had gone!

On a happier note, Vic Loveless recalled the outstanding success of the Association's Annual Dinner at Beaulieu 'Domus', when David Barter and Fred Trueman were in top form as after-dinner speakers.

The New Year of 1985 was greeted at Townhill Park by the thirteenth annual playing of 1st of January cricket, on this occasion Ralph Coney's XI defeating Eccentrics. The season proper offered a familiar combination of wind and rain, against which the county side, captained by Mark Nicholas, challenged strongly for all four trophies contested.

Of considerable interest in 1985, Hursley Park's bi-centenary publication *200 Years of Cricket in Hursley* told of the club's achievements over the years, culminating in an appearance at Lord's in the 1984 Whitbread Village Cricket Championship Final, where the Hampshire club went down to Marchwiel by just 8 runs. The winners made 159 for 7 (T. Roberts 55), Hursley Park 151 for 8 (Adrian Aymes 56). Hursley Park were Hampshire League Division One champions for 1985.

Histories such as Hursley Park's, as with the variety of handbook publications throughout the county, form an invaluable source of cricket information. Hampshire County Cricket Club's 1986 handbook, edited by Tony Mitchener, paid a number of tributes, including that to Peter Marshall who had edited the handbook for the previous eight years. Tony Mitchener acknowledged valued assistance from Vic Isaacs (statistics), Mike Taylor (advertising). Patrick Eagar (photographs), and David O'Brien (printing). Cecil Paris, Hampshire C.C.C. President, wrote in warm appreciation of the work that retiring Chairman (Geoffrey Ford) and Secretary (A.K. 'Jimmy' James) had carried out not only within the county but on the wider scene also.

As well as factual information, handbooks often contain individual and team photographs. Group pictures in cricket's past have with many clubs been taken on an as-and-when basis, often with gaps of ten years or more. Faces and names are important to the archives of cricket. Annual publications during the 1970s and 1980s went some way towards putting right such omissions, certainly so far as the present time was concerned. The Hampshire Cricket League Handbook for 1986, like others, a quality production, gave much interesting information about the league's leading performers, Colin Thresher of Bishop's Waltham, for instance, having to date more than 550 wicketkeeping dismissals during his Hampshire League career. In welcoming Rowledge to the league, the handbook outlined the outstanding success of Rowledge in the l'Anson League and National Village competition.

The Hampshire Cricket League in 1986 again saw a number of names new to recent title claims, among them Follands, Crofton (in the now formed County Division Four), Old Edwardians, Ellingham, Medstead and Rowledge. The Save and Prosper Southern League had two fresh names for its honours list, South Hants Touring Club winning the Senior Division, Waterlooville taking the 2nd IX Championship. Conscious of the need to improve the standard of wickets, the league organized an April 1987 groundsman's seminar at Hurn, in conjunction with Peter Dury and Christchurch Borough Council. The cover of the *Hampshire Handbook* for 1987 told the county's main story for the 1986 season: a colour photo by Murray Sanders showing Hampshire skipper Mark Nicholas lifting on high the John Player Special League Trophy. 'King for a Day' was used to sum up Hampshire wicketkeeper Bob Parks's experience in putting on the England gloves against India at Lord's, following injury to 'keeper Bruce French. Bob Parks tells of learning of the call-up from a 10.30 a.m. phone call at home by Hampshire Chief Executive Tony Baker. At first Bob wondered 'Could it be a Tremlett prank'; only listening to the car radio at 11 o'clock was he convinced that he was on his way to take over from Bob Taylor, one of those temporarily holding the fort.

The Cricket Memorabilia Society's formation in April 1987 owed much to the inspiration of Don Crossley of Chandler's Ford. The summer 1987 Hampshire Cricket Society Newsletter number 100 (the first issue having appeared during 1976) came in a season when the M.C.C. was celebrating its bi-centenary. In the M.C.C.'s 200 years' history, Hampshire had often played a key role.

Longparish in 1987 became the first Hampshire side to win a one-day competition at Lord's, defeating Treeton Welfare from South Yorkshire in the National Village Club Final, sponsored by Norsk Hydro Fertilisers. Longparish made 166 (John Heagren 63) from 39.5 overs, then dismissed Treeton Welfare for 90, 3 wickets each for Smith and Sturt. Longparish were also in close contention with Hampshire League Division One winners Hursley Park, a competition in which Fareham, with Portsmouth & Southsea, maintained their record of having appeared in the top division each season since the league's 1973 formation.

The Save and Prosper Southern League, happily immune from much of the adverse weather clouding other parts of the country, had South Hants Touring Club, Jon Ayling prominent with bat and ball, retaining the senior title. Bournemouth took the 2nd XI championship. Havant batsman Paul Gover was chosen as the league's 'Young Cricketer of the Year' for 1987. Past winners, from 1981, encouraged by Messrs Holt and Haskell of Southampton, had been Neil Moseley (Winchester), Tony Middleton (Trojans), Nigel Ackland (Bournemouth), Richard Scott (Bournemouth), Neil Taylor (New Milton), Jon Ayling (South Hants T.C.). Close on the heels of the 1987 season, indoor competitions such as Farley's South Hampshire League at Eastleigh's Fleming Park Leisure Centre, and the Hammond Jewellers Colts League, were under way in the autumn.

As with other seasons in Hampshire's past, 1988 provided plenty for team and individual memory. Isle of Wight cricket continued actively at varied levels. In the Morey's League tables, Brading were Division One winners, Westover winners of the 2nd division, and Whitecroft Division Three winners. Newport won the Bill Palmer Memorial League, Ryde the Six-a-side Cup, and Arreton the Six-a-side Plate. In the leading Leisure Indoor League 1988-9, unbeaten Newport were Division One champions.

Hampshire's 1988 colts, managed by Barry Reed, reached the Esso Oxford N.A.Y.C. Final for the second successive season. Skipper Rory Macleay, Sean Morris and Charles Forward succeeded with the bat; Darren Flint and Mark Copping were well among the wickets. Derek Pepperell, in 1989 to become a prolific Southern League batsman with Bournemouth, kept wicket to a high standard.

Hampshire School's Cricket Association depended, as throughout the years, on individual dedication to ensure that provision was made for players of the future. The award of a C.B.E. to President, Cyril Cooper, was in recognition of outstanding services to this area of the game. The Association continued to be indebted to contributors such as Secretary Michael May.

At senior level, Paultons in 1988 became the ninth club in sixteen seasons to take the Hampshire League Division One title. Basics-Polhill, the only team among ten divisions to remain unbeaten in 1988, were Division Two leaders, and with runners-up Hale were promoted to Division One for the first time. The League Representative XI were beaten semi-finalists in the Famous Grouse Inter-League competition. The 1988 Famous Grouse title was taken by the Save and Prosper Southern League with a 23-run win over Beach Villas Three Counties League. Winchester, captained by Rob Savage, became Southern League 1988 champions, with Bournemouth claiming the 2nd XI title.

Justin Jackman (R.A.P.C., Worthy Down) with 150 against the Fire Service set up a new Wiltshier League record, a competition won in 1988 by Owslebury. Also on the record trail during 1988, Chris Bazalgette became only the second player in Hampshire Hogs' history to reach 500 wickets, although having some way to go in pursuit of F.G. Irving's 750 total. On the Sunday scene, Bishopstoke

S.C. retained the Eastleigh League title, as well as defeating runners-up Wayfarers in the Eastleigh Sunday League Cup Final.

Hampshire County XI's 1988 season was memorable for winning the Benson and Hedges Cup Final at Lord's. Steve Jefferies (5 wickets for 13) with vital runs from captain Mark Nicholas and Robin Smith, played a key part in a low-scoring contest with Derbyshire.

Braving New Year's Day 1989 winter chill, public house regulars Buck's Head Gumbles defeated Meonstoke cricketers (dressed as women) in a match that raised funds for the Great Ormond Street Children's Hospital appeal. The summer of 1989 would prove to be one of the hottest and sunniest within memory of almost all cricketers. Taking full advantage, Hampshire cricket at all levels built up towards some thrilling late-season climaxes.

Steve Malone's 51 wickets played a major part in the achievement of Old Tauntonians becoming Save and Prosper Southern League champions. Old Tauntonians were also runners-up to leaders Bournemouth in the 2nd XI Championship. In New Forest Division One, Wadham Stringer sponsored, Calmore won all eighteen matches. On the Isle of Wight, Northwood became Bill Palmer Memorial League title holders, Peter Came's 99 playing a key role in a late season decider against a close rivals Ventnor, for whom Jeff Hose made a rapid 50.

Hambledon's visit to Lord's for the Hydro Village Cricket Championship Final, contested at the start by some 630 teams, ended in anti-climax. Having made 72 for 5 against Toft at Lord's before rain ended Saturday play, Hambledon had the opportunity of a next day re-start, at Beckenham. On the second occasion Hambledon made 104, to lose by 6 wickets. The county side tasted bitter defeat in the Nat West Trophy semi-final at Southampton, when, seemingly well poised to pass Middlesex's 267 for 7 off 60 overs, Hampshire's century-maker Chris Smith suffered a broken thumb that virtually ended his effectiveness and allowed Middlesex back into the game.

With clearly joyful memories of 1989, Lawrie Scott for C.L.C. Charendon in Southampton's Lawson Tools Parks League made 279 (28 sixes, 19 fours) of his side's 427 for 1 versus Hendy Ford, sharing an opening 427 in 32 overs with Stewart Shapland (138 not out). Hampshire's 'Golden Oldies' had an enjoyable 1989 in the N.C.A. 50-plus Championship, winning three of their six group matches, Mike Chauffourier and Howard Wright-Green among the runs, John Rickard the most successful bowler. At the younger end, colts XIs throughout the county strove away at their own competitions, some of which were played on Sunday mornings, often under the supervision of parents and others who had already spent Saturdays committed to cricket.

Basingstoke & North Hants became *Echo* trophy holders, defeating Hambledon on a late July evening at Southampton County Ground. Basingstoke's 125 for 6 off 22 overs owed much to 60 from Ray Pavesi, batting in distinctive duck-egg blue pads. Then with the ball Ray Pavesi took 5 for 23 to restrict Hambledon to 104 for 7 from their allotted 22 overs.

Club dinners and presentation evenings would during the close season of 1989-90, as in the past, form an eagerly awaited part of cricket. Hampshire is fortunate in having a number of speakers well worth listening to. County players such as Chris Smith, Bob Parks and Tim Tremlett are among those to have been particularly successful at colts functions. Others to have graced league and club occasions have been Peter Roebuck, Peter Parfitt, Mark Nicholas, Micky Stewart, Brian Johnston, Arthur Holt, Fred Trueman, 'Bomber' Wells, Ken Suttle, Mike Taylor, Cecil Paris and Nick Pocock. Burley's Presentation Evening of February 1987 had been special in that presenting the trophies was George Ashby, who had recently completed fifty years as a player with Christchurch in the Bournemouth League.

Cricket periodicals in and out of season provide much to interest followers of both the club and first-class scene. *Cricket World* in its 1989 lists of Foster's Century Award winners contained a number of Hampshire names. Among those to feature were Mick Holland (Shanklin), Marke Whyte (Ventnor), David Porter and Tim Simmonite (both of Shanklin), with other clubs to appear including Hursley Park, King's Somborne, Romsey, Hambledon and United Services Portsmouth.

The August 1989 issue of *Cricket World* contained William J. Drinkwater's thoughts on Hampshire cricketers commemorated on cigarette cards of the past, ranging from Harry Baldwin to Sam Pothecary. Jim Danks of Portsmouth drew November 1989 *Cricket World*'s attention to father, brother and son of the Izzard family having a part in each of the ten Portsmouth Grammar School batsmen dismissals against United Services Portsmouth.

Hampshire County Council in 1989 commemorated its centenary. Gillian A. Rushton told of *100 Years of Progress* in a publication of much fascination. Of the county council officers listed, Hampshire's first County Librarian, Mr H.M. Sherry, had been a keen club cricketer in his years with Castle C.C. Hampshire's County Architect from 1973 has been Mr C. Stansfield-Smith C.B.E., himself a cricketer of note. Colin Stansfield-Smith won a Blue in each of his four seasons at Cambridge University, and between 1951 and 1957 played for Lancashire, on occasions partnering Brian Statham in Lancashire's opening attack.

Peter Wynne-Thomas had, in *The History of Hampshire Cricket Club*, taken the club's story up to 1987. Future historians will have much to write about first-class and other levels in years to come. The 1980s had been for Hampshire cricket a full and absorbing decade. There had been changes taking place within the game, some obvious, others more subtle. Minds had during 1989 begun to turn themselves towards the 1990s, a decade likely to be of importance in a number of ways.

12

Into the Future

CRICKET'S PRESENT AND FUTURE are closely related to the past, particularly in Hampshire, where ambitious growth is planned for the 1990s. Many clubs within the county are committed to the development of grounds and off-the-field facilities. The County Cricket Club plans, to move from its Southampton Headquarters at Northlands Road to a site at West End, will mean a major break with the past.

Concern with the past is a feature of forward planning at many levels. A number of club histories published in recent years have their origins in a wish to examine and expand. Hampshire County Cricket Club's Curator, Neil Jenkinson, is already active in preparing material for a museum to be included in the new County Ground complex. Within the county, men such as Doug Welsh, with some half a century at Portsmouth's United Services Ground, and Stan Foster, with decades of service to the Hook and Newnham Club, have been able to pass on knowledge gained over the years. Southampton Parks cricket has been indebted to people like Gerry Le Brocq.

Alive to the county's past as well as the present, the Hampshire Cricket Society is during 1990 carrying out research into the history of various Hampshire grounds. Through its regular newsletters the society (patrons John Arlott and John Woodcock) is able to evoke the past and stimulate the present. Newsletter contributors such as Alan Edwards, E.M. Wellings, Mike Arnold, Don Crossley (active nationally in the world of cricket memorabilia), Tony Mitchener and Frank Bailey have ensured an always lively and readable bulletin. By way of meetings throughout the county, the Hampshire Cricket Society has enabled members and guests to share the recollections and predictions of many whose names feature prominently in Hampshire cricket. Speakers in recent years have included John Holder, Malcolm Heath, Bob Parks, Mike Barnard, Patrick Eagar, Nick Pocock and John Hughes. Quiz evenings provide opportunities to test the skills of contestants such as Trevor Jesty, Keith Stevenson, Paul Terry, Bill Leadbetter, Freddie Houldsworth and Peter Collop, together with the timekeeping of Pam Gerrard.

The Hampshire Exiles, as well as supporting the county club at home and abroad, encourage coming generations with an annual award which, since its inauguration in 1978, has recognized the young promise of Hampshire players such as Tim Tremlett, Malcolm Marshall, Kevin Emery, Cardigan Connor, Rajesh Maru and Stephen Andrew.

Hampshire cricket is rich in literature and illustration, to which newspapers dating back to the *Hampshire Chronicle* in 1772 have made a unique contribution. Adding greatly to the pictorial record is Patrick Eagar, of strong Hampshire connection, whose cricket photography has won international acclaim. Recently issued sound cassettes allow us to share the absorbing reminiscences of former Hampshire captain Colin Ingleby-Mackenzie, and to relish an anthology of John Arlott's memorable broadcasting. The County Cricket Club's scorer and statistician Victor Isaacs has worked endlessly to collate and preserve figures necessary to an accurate record of the Hampshire team throughout its history.

Important to the future of Hampshire cricket, there are men and women willing to use for the benefit of younger generations the experience they have gained over the years. Such qualities are valuable in umpiring and scoring. Hampshire has now around a dozen local umpiring associations, with people such as Mrs M. Hennessy, Clem Dymond, Tony Leadbetter, Ray Flood, Alan Orbell, Tom Dexter, John Hardy, Eric Effemey, Brian Pardey and Steve Judd among those to contribute fully.

The ranks of players and administrators have many with commendable records of service on and off the field, who have been prepared to remain active contributors. From various areas of involvement might be named Wifrid Weld (president of Hampshire County Cricket Club in 1990), Jean Anderson, Eric Noble, John Rickard, Stan Rudder, Don Whitlock, Robin Johns, Robert Turner, Dave Galpin, Donald Rich, Margaret Bailey, Brian White, Lew Gregory, Barbara Luff and John Harris. Still much concerned with the game are former Hampshire cricketers Jimmy Gray, Peter Sainsbury, Barry Reed, Alan Wassell, Bob Herman, Peter Haslop and Derek Tulk, while through Radio Solent broadcasts we have access to the informed opinions of Mike Barnard and Neville Rogers. Present-day all-rounder Kevan James, and the County's 1990 prized acquisition David Gower, provide press comment that takes us interestingly inside the sometimes exclusive world of professional cricket.

Into the 1990s there are young cricketers at school, colts and club level whose names are already beginning to catch newspaper headlines. It will be interesting to follow the careers of James West, David Blizzard, Charles Forward, Derek Pepperell, Neil Champion, Greg Lewis, Patrick Dearden, Jeremy Hayes, Mark Garroway and Steve Pinder. Important to their future is the opportunity to play on good wickets. From county level (where Hampshire's Tom Flintoft has won high reputation) to village green, the value of a true surface cannot be over estimated. Some years ago a former Hampshire stalwart, Jack Newman, said that 'If you don't have good practice wickets, use the square'. A number of clubs follow that policy. The county side in 1990 has a number of younger players -

Richard Scott, Ian Turner, Tony Middleton, Adrian Aymes, Jonathon Ayling, Kevin Shine and Julian Wood - vying to take their place in the team alongside such established names as Chris Smith, skipper Mark Nicholas, Robin Smith, Malcolm Marshall, David Gower and Paul Terry.

Young and older alike will during the 1990s be part of a game that is changing. There will be increasing emphasis on the value of sponsorship at all levels. Indoor competitions will continue to keep cricket alive durng the winter; more and more clubs are investing in non-turf wickers, for match use as well as practice. Colts cricket may increasingly fill a regretted gap left by the reduced participation from a number of schools. There will be opportunity to make cricket history at both ends of the scale. During the 1990s Save and Prosper Southern League Second Eleven League season, Alton reached a total of 302 for 4, then a few weeks later were dismissed for 0 (albeit batting with one man short through injury) by Bournemouth 2nd XI, Ash Niak taking 5 for 0, Alan Hayden 4 for 0. In the New Forest League Division Two, Phil Craymer for Exbury against Romey during July 1990 achieved the rare club feat of a double century, making 234 not out.

League and cup competitions came very much to the fore during the 1980s, with a number of clubs finding it increasingly difficult to field adequate elevens for Sunday 'friendly' fixtures. Club tours, of up to a week at a time, abroad on occasions, have become fashionable once more. The Hampshire Cricket Association (Chairman, Bill Fielder) called a January 1990 meeting with a view to bringing together the various leagues with which Hampshire clubs are involved. A steering committee meeting was formed with the aim of establishing by the mid 1990s a pyramid system of promotion and relegation between the various leagues. The purpose of such change is to bring about an overall improvement of cricketing standards. In agreement with the long-term aims of integration were the Save and Prosper Southern League, the Wiltshier Winchester League, the New Forest Wadham Stringer League, the North Hants League, the Southdown League and the Solent League, together with delegates from the Three Counties League (serving Berkshire, Hampshire and Surrey).

With levels of competition being raised all round, captaincy becomes important in a way not always required in the past. At club and representative standard, players of the quality of Neil Trestrail, Mike Edwards, Paul Gover, Paul Rogers and Ian Wilkins have to meet increasing demands. County cricket has moved towards the appointment of managers, a role carried out in Somerset by Hampshire opponent of many past occasions, Jack Birkenshaw, who has in his charge former Hampshire batsman Jon Hardy, a powerful hitter of the ball. Hampshire's own administration was for many seasons past headed by a secretary. Tony Baker's present title of Chief Executive reflects the increasing business element of that role.

Of all those connected with Hampshire's cricketing past, former player and

County President, Harry Altham, was particularly concerned not only with the richness of history but also with the encouragement of young cricketers. Among his reminiscences, written in the 1960s, Harry Altham asked of cricket the question 'And why do we love it as we do, and want those who come after us to love it too?' In answer to his own question he replied '...because as long as it is true to itself it offers us rewards that cannot stale, and stands for values that in a changing world remain unchanged.'

If Hampshire cricket wishes words to take it from the past into the future, those of Harry Altham seem particularly apt.

Bibliography

'Aesop' (pseud.) *Sporting Reminiscences of Hampshire from 1745 to 1862* (Chapman and Hall, 1864)

Altham, Harry; Arlott, John; Eagar, Desmond; Webber, Roy *The Official History of Hampshire County Cricket Club* (Phoenix Sports Books, 1957)

Arlott, John (ed.) *From Hambledon to Lord's: The Classics of Cricket* (Barry Shurlock, 1948)

Ashley-Cooper, F. S. *The Hambledon Cricket Chronicle 1772-1796* (Herbert Jenkins 1924)

Bailey, P; Thorn, P; Wynne-Thomas, P. *Who's Who of Cricketers* (Newnes Books in association with the Association of Cricket Statisticians, 1984)

Bettey, J. H. *Wessex from A.D. 1000* (Longman, 1986)

Biddlecombe, Ron *Cadnam Cricket Club 1880-1980* (Cadnam C.C., 1980)

Brookes, Christopher *English Cricket: The Game and Its Players through the Ages* (Weidenfeld & Nicolson, 1978)

Burt, Ian R. *Froxfield Cricket Club* (Froxfield C.C., 1979)

Edwards, Alan *Milestones of Hampshire Cricket* (Hampshire Cricket Society 1983)

Fellowes, Edmund H. *A History of Winchester Cricket* (Messrs P. & G. Wells, 1930)

Ford, John *Cricket: A Social History 1700-1835* (David & Charles, 1972)

Goulstone, John *Early Club & Village Cricket* (1972)

Hampshire County Cricket Club: Annual Handbooks

Hampshire Cricket Society: Newsletters

Harrison, B.R.S. and Bichard, P.M. *Basingstoke and North Hants Cricket Club, 1865-1965* (Basingstoke & North Hants C.C. c 1966)

Hursley Park C. C. *200 Years of Cricket in Hursley* (Hursley Park C.C., 1985)

Ingleby-Mackenzie, Colin *Many a Slip* (Oldbourne, 1962)

Jarrett, David *England in the Age of Hogarth* (Hart-Davis 1974)

Kelly, Tom *The Cricket Cubs of Christchurch* (Kelly, c 1988)

Lucas, E. V. *The Hambledon Men* (Phoenix House, 1907, reprinted 1954)

Martineau, G. D. *Bat, Ball, Wicket and All* (Sporting Handbooks, 1950)

Martin-Jenkins, Christopher (ed.) *Cricket's Lighter Side* (Simon & Schuster, 1988)

Mason, Ronald *Sing All a Green Willow* (Epworth Press, 1967)

Mate, Charles H. and Riddle, Charles *Bournemouth 1810-1910* (W Mate 1910)

Mathew, Robert 'De Collegio', poem in *Magdalen MS* (1647)

May, John *Cricket in North Hants*(Warren, 1906)

Mitford, Mary Russell 'The Cricket Match', in the *Lady's Magazine* (1823)

Montgomery, F. J. *Deanery Cricket Club* (1921)

Norris, A. C. *Two Centuries of Beaulieu Cricket: 1775-1975* (A. C. Norris, c. 1979)

Nyren, John *The Young Cricketer's Tutor* and *The Cricketers of My Time*, ed. Charles Cowsen Clarke (1833)

Patterson, A. Temple *A History of Southampton 1700-1914* (Vol. 1) (Southampton University 1966)

Pawson, Tony *Runs and Catches* (Faber & Faber, 1980)

Phillips, Edward 'The Mysteries of Love', poem quoted in Martineau, G. D. (see above)

Pycroft, Revd James *The Cricket Field* (1851)

Rowley, Simon *Burley C.C. Centenary Year Handbook, 1875-1975* (Burley C.C., 1975)

Rushton, Gillian A. *100 Years of Progress: Hampshire County Council 1889-1975* (Hampshire County Council, 1989)

Smith, Doug *The Origins of Cricket: the History of Two Hampshire clubs* [Odiham and Greywell] (Odiham C.C., 1980)

Sporting Magazine, 1819

Swanton, E.W.; Woodcock, J.; Plumtre, G.; Winslaw, A.S. R.; Copinger, G.A. *Barclays World of Cricket* (Collins with Barclays Bank, 2nd ed. 1980)

Webb, Ken and Loose, John *Bramshaw Cricket Club, 1877-1977* (Bramshaw C.C. 1977)

Webber, Roy *The County Cricket Championship* (Phoenix, 1957)

Wisden's Cricketers' Almanack, various years

Wooldridge, Ian *Travelling Reserve* (Collins, 1982)

Wynne-Thomas, Peter *The History of Hampshire County Cricket Club* (Christopher Helm, 1989)

Selected Index